"This dynamic book doesn't just describe from on high the increasingly interim nature of work in today's economy. *A New Brand of Expertise* draws from the experience of a key player aiding the transition, and will be of invaluable help to anyone trying to work in the new economy."

—Tom Ehrenfeld, author, *The Startup Garden: How Growing a Business Grows You*

"Independent consulting as a lifestyle and career choice is destined to thrive as another force shaping the new economy. In *A New Brand of Expertise*, Marion McGovern and M², the leading talent agent for independent consultants, share industry insights of value to both companies and individuals who are readying to catch the wave."

—Martin Babinec, Chairman and CEO, TriNet

"Marion McGovern knows what it takes to add value in today's zip-zap world of commerce. After all, she was among the early visionaries who not only predicted the 'free agent nation' and the globalized 'new economy,' she literally helped *shape* them! *A New Brand of Expertise* is long-awaited wisdom from the source."

—Dr. Louis Patler, author, *TILT! Irreverent Lessons for Leading Innovation in the New Economy*

"The authors deftly guide the reader through the 'white-water' of hiring or becoming an independent consultant. I was fascinated by this book, and speed-read it from cover to cover! I heartily recommend it to any company considering retaining an interim manager or independent consultant, and to anyone interested in pursuing an independent career."

—Lorin Letendre, Chairman, CPP

"This easy-to-read and example-rich treatise on whether and how to join the ranks of freelance consultants is a must-read primer for anyone contemplating becoming an independent or using one. From IRS regs to the role of veracity, from deliverables to pricing, McGovern and Russell cover all the basics of this new way to work. I strongly recommend *A New Brand of Expertise* to new and seasoned practitioners."

—Peter Yessne, Publisher and President,
Staffing Industry Analysts, Inc.

"*A New Brand of Expertise* provides the free agent worker with the enormous experience that McGovern and M^2 have developed over the years in serving the market for project-based work. It's good advice. Listen to it."

—William Bridges, author, *Creating You & Co.*

"M^2 makes my job easier! Our clients need access to the best consulting and interim executive talent in the Silicon Valley—fast. Free agents like those you will meet in *A New Brand of Expertise* are one of the few resources we can count on to deliver this critical expertise to our portfolio companies."

—Teri McFadden, Senior Recruiting Partner,
Accel Partners

"In *A New Brand of Expertise*, Marion McGovern presents her flexible staffing business model, which extends the concept of ecosystem partnering to the individual level. If any company desires to create a sustainable strategy for human capital, I would strongly suggest that they consider her model."

—John Sifonis, author, *Net Ready*

"*A New Brand of Expertise* is filled with valuable advice for both clients and consultants. Marion McGovern and her company, M^2, are really experts in this space, and the book reflects their years of experience."

—Teri Dial, President and CEO,
Wells Fargo Bank, California

A NEW BRAND OF EXPERTISE:

How Independent Consultants,
Free Agents, and Interim Managers
Are Transforming the World of Work

A
NEW BRAND
OF EXPERTISE:

How Independent Consultants,
Free Agents, and Interim Managers Are
Transforming the World of Work

Marion McGovern

Dennis Russell

BUTTERWORTH
HEINEMANN

Boston   Oxford   Auckland   Johannesburg   Melbourne   New Delhi

♾ Recognizing the importance of preserving what has been written, Butterworth–Heinemann prints its books on acid-free paper whenever possible.

 Butterworth–Heinemann supports the efforts of American Forests and the Global ReLeaf program in its campaign for the betterment of trees, forests, and our environment.

Library of Congress Cataloging-in-Publication Data

McGovern, Marion, 1958–
  A new brand of expertise : how independent consultants, free agents, and
  interim managers are transforming the world of work / by Marion
  McGovern, Dennis Russell.
    p. cm.
  Includes index.
  ISBN 0-7506-7292-7 (paperback : alk. paper)
  1. Interim executives. 2. Management. I. Russell, Dennis. II. Title.
  HD38.23 .M38 2000
  658.4—dc21   00-060860

British Library Cataloguing-in-Publication Data

A catalogue record for this book is available from the British Library.

The publisher offers special discounts on bulk orders of this book.

For information, please contact:

Manager of Special Sales
Butterworth–Heinemann
225 Wildwood Avenue
Woburn, MA 01801–2041
Tel: 781-904-2500
Fax: 781-904-2620

For information on all Butterworth–Heinemann publications available, contact our World Wide Web home page at: http://www.bh.com

10 9 8 7 6 5 4 3 2 1

Printed in the United States of America

For my husband, Jerry, and my children, Morgan, Nora, and Kevin, who continually shape my perspective on time, life, and the future

MM

TABLE OF CONTENTS

FOREWORD

Early in 1992 I was made redundant for the fourth time in my life. This time around, with a fine irony, it was from an outplacement agency, where I had been a regional director for four years. Needless to say I was well counseled by my ex-colleagues on what to do next, and I began work as an independent marketing consultant. Casting about for assignments after a few months, I met Carl Hague, who had recently founded one of the earliest interim management agencies in the UK. We began a fruitful partnership that lasted until I retired in 1997. During those years we struck a lot of sparks off one another, and did a lot to invent and refine the concept of Interim Management. We stated very firmly that Interim Management is *not* working temporarily at one job while you are waiting for the next "proper" job to come along. That's a perfectly sensible thing to do on occasion of course, but we labeled that "Temporary Management," and actually tended to exclude such people from our portfolio. By "Interim Managers," we meant those who had made a *career choice* to be independent, generating income from a series of contracts—for example, a consultancy analysis for one organization, a training course produced for a second, and an interim (or locum) management job for a third. Sometimes all three at the same time! What the Interim Manager does is, we felt, less important than the *terms* under which the Interim Manager works—most commonly paid by the day.

We named our agency "Praxis," a word of Greek origin meaning "accepted custom or practice." Like our rapidly burgeoning competitors, we thrived in the UK's open economy. And the best part of the job was meeting, day after day, the Interim Managers who earned our modest fees for us. We found them to be, collectively and individually, a hugely impressive resource that year by year became more effective with each assignment carried out. So when I decided to write "the book," it was natural for me to turn to some of the many friends I had made to ask them the important questions: How did you become an Interim Manager? What do you enjoy—and hate— about the life? What do you wish you had known before starting out, now that you have learned by painful experience?

The answers, interwoven with my own insights and analysis, make up the UK publication *Interim Management*—you will find it on Internet booksellers' Websites if you are interested!

One thing I was sure of was that I had written a very personal book, strongly embedded in our UK-based experience. As such, I thought it unlikely that it would have all the answers for the USA, which I knew would be the biggest market in the world for the right book on the subject. I had worked in North America for a couple of years, and I am also blessed with an American son-in-law *and* an American daughter-in-law. I had no difficulty in discovering that things are different in the USA!

So I looked at agencies in the US similar to Praxis, and came across a press story about M^2. I talked myself into Marion McGovern's office in downtown San Francisco while on a visit. Marion and her team enjoyed my book, and agreed that I had laid a useful foundation, but felt that things really were starting to diverge in American practice, particularly regarding the impact of the Internet, which was already significant on the West Coast but hardly visible in the UK. So I struck up another delightful partnership, giving Marion *carte blanche* to make sweeping changes to the contents of my book to suit the US market. I think she's done a great job. Any employer considering using independents will gain hugely from her analysis and sound advice—and certainly no independent should set out without it.

A final quotation from my favorite lines of poetry:

> Out of the night that covers me
> Black as the pit from pole to pole
> I thank whatever Gods may be
> For my unconquerable soul

> —*William Henley*

That's my idea of a good battle hymn for the Interim Manager. Good luck!

Dennis Russell
Salcombe, England
Autumn, 2000

PREFACE

Twelve years ago, I founded M^2 as a firm in the business of brokering independent consultants. A former management consultant myself, I recognized that the traditional consulting firm mode of smart young MBAs who didn't really understand a client's business was not always the best option for the client. Indeed, an individual who really understood the issue, industry, or opportunity may be the better solution to that urgent business problem. With that epiphany, M^2 was founded and, in retrospect, was on the crest of a wave of change sweeping through organizations and society.

In its early years, the struggle was credibility. We were evangelists, preaching the value of individual experts who could solve problems cost-effectively. A typical response back then was: "Who are these people? They must just be unemployed," or "Why would I want them to work for me if they can't get a REAL job?"

Ironically, the people who were independent consultants in the late 1980s were consummate professionals. Independent consulting is like speculating. Good speculators make money and continue, whereas bad speculators lose all of their capital and need to do something else. In the same way: good consultants can make a tremendous living, whereas those who are less successful often need to close their doors and go back to regular work. The people who were successful in the 1980s at a time when few companies recognized the power of this kind of approach were truly world-class consultants.

Over time, our message seemed less foreign. The massive corporate restructuring of the early 1990s prompted cover stories in *Fortune* and *Forbes* magazines about the new "executive temps." We were repeatedly interviewed by the media to discuss and decry the temping of America. Although concern about the contingent workforce became increasingly politically charged, our lone voice suggested that this new free agent or independent consultant represented the silver lining in what was perceived to be a dark cloud, because these individuals were independent by choice and were creating a new entrepreneurial lifestyle.

The trend has only continued—as it will in the future—as changing organizational models begin to take hold in large and small companies. What we notice now is growing diversity in the ranks of the free agents. We still see the senior executive with 20 years or more of experience in an industry hanging out his or her shingle for any one of several reasons. This seasoned manager knows how to turn around enterprises, motivate client employees, and launch new initiatives. But now, with the rise of the "e" world, we see a younger, more technically savvy individual entrepreneur, more visionary than managerial, who is interested in building a body of work through independent consulting activities. Both types of consultant are valuable in today's market. The task for intermediaries like M^2 is to discern which type is best for the client.

Similarly, the diversity in our client base is growing. What was once a resource for large enterprises constrained by headcount freezes or determined to move more quickly than a competitor has now become an option, or in some cases an imperative, for small, high-growth companies as well.

This book is a labor of love because I love this new industry that M^2 helped create. It is intended to empower our partners, the consultants and clients with whom we work. Independent consulting is by definition a lonely business. M^2 seeks to build a sense of community with these high-powered individuals. The more we can help them launch, maintain, and grow their practices, the more business we can do together.

Similarly, many of our newer clients are not knowledgeable about how to bring in spot expertise. We work with them to develop the appropriate measurable deliverables, but understanding the difference between expert free agents and employees is a key factor of success for companies. The more we can help our client companies be successful, the more we can grow their business and ours.

This book is laced with anecdotes derived from our more than a dozen years in pioneering this business. (If I seem to be shamelessly promoting M^2, I apologize. Feel free to assume that other companies would have similar stories.) We include these examples as a key to the future; to truly understand the future, we need to appreciate the past. The consultants who are profiled are real people, although some are so colorful that they may seem fictitious. One of the joys of being in a people business is that you constantly rediscover how truly fascinating people can be. This is especially true of people who are pursuing their ideal and creating a career that offers intellectual challenge, financial reward, and time for a life in between. Our goal as a company is to empower independent management talent. We hope that, through this book, you will sense the sheer power and reward that comes from that fulfillment.

This book was written with a wide audience in mind. For company executives who may not be accustomed to deploying this new brand of expertise, this book can serve as a framework for a best-practices approach to strategy. For those who have shunned this method to date, perhaps this will provide the wake-up call to announce that the world has changed, and those who do not learn to effectively utilize these exceptional independent consultants may find their businesses eclipsed by those who do. For tried and true "consumers" of independent talent, their strategies will be validated and they will be exposed to a plethora of ways other companies have creatively utilized these resources, providing these readers with great new ideas for their own businesses. Part I and Part III should be of greatest interest for these readers.

For individuals who are considering this new way of life, this book should offer some guidance on how to go about making the transition. Part II should be especially on point for those just starting out. Experienced consultants like those we profile within could read it for their own edification. Although, by definition, much of the content directed toward consultants may already be known to them, there may be some nuance that can add value to already successful practitioners.

Finally, it is my ultimate goal that all readers come away with a clear appreciation for how the capital markets are shifting, as intellectual capital is now becoming a mobile asset. As economists will attest, the free flow of capital is a prerequisite to an efficient market. In our lifetime, we will witness the free flow of human capital, the beginnings of which this book chronicles. It is exciting to ponder the impact of this trend on all of us in terms of the efficiency improvements for business, as well as the equally beneficial impact on our quality of life.

Marion McGovern

ACKNOWLEDGMENTS

Having now written this book, I truly appreciate the Acknowledgments page. I admit that I have often skipped over it, seeing it as a rather internally focused appendage. Now I understand how profoundly important this section can be, when so much effort and support goes into a book. In the words of Hillary Clinton, "It takes a village," not just to raise a child, but to write a book.

Certainly, *A New Brand of Expertise* would not have happened had it not been for Dennis Russell and his predecessor book, *Interim Management.* As I recall the day we spent comparing and contrasting our respective businesses when Dennis happened to be in northern California on holiday, I never thought our conversations would lead to this endeavor. I recall only being so fascinated at how the same fundamental business need could drive very different business models, where the primary source of the variance was culturally derived. Thanks, Dennis, not only for writing your book, but also for visiting with me that day, because that formed the basis for our relationship.

Stepping back even further, it is certainly my company, M^2, that has afforded me the insight into and knowledge of this new breed of workers. M^2 has always had a dual constituency: the companies who trust us with their business problems and the consultants who offer to provide solutions to them. Serving those clients over the years has educated me about this marketplace and its priorities, constraints, and idiosyncrasies. Perhaps I have learned the most from those clients who come back to us on a regular basis for additional spot expertise to address their urgent business needs. For those companies, such as Wells Fargo, Charles Schwab, Accel Partners, and Kaiser Permanente, to name a few, I can only say thank you.

Many people provided important content to the work. The 22 consultants who contributed quotes are certainly high on the list. Without their input, the motivations of this new brand of expertise would not have seemed as alive. In addition, there were many others in the M^2 consulting network who offered their views, but who may not have been quoted directly. Sometimes this was because I had already referenced a similar sentiment, so I hope when those individuals read the book they will hear resonating viewpoints. In other cases, some were too busy with clients or holidays to respond in time, which demonstrates the essence of this new lifestyle. Nonetheless, I appreciate all of your efforts and thank you for your thoughts. Also, I thank Guru.com for pitching in on a tight deadline with the sidebar about the impact of the Internet space on this arena.

The M^2 team was also a large part of the heart and soul of this effort. Many of our veteran managers, such as MaryAnn Malinak, VP of Growth and Development, and Lori Perlstadt, Senior VP of Marketing and Sales, supplied not only ideas and editorial assistance but moral support as well. A special thanks goes to Elizabeth Charney, a former M^2 employee, who agreed to pitch in and lend her expertise to some of the scripting of the book. My partners, Paula Reynolds and Claire McAuliffe, were invaluable in sustaining the creative muse to complete the book. They know that our efforts in building this company certainly created insights to fill at least one book—if not several. Ladies, the next books will have to wait.

Finally, I want to thank my family. My mother, Phyllis Blaum, not only was a willing reader, but also now understands what my company does. In fact, she read the manuscript on a plane, where she had bad service, and concluded that the airline needed a consultant to solve its problems. My children, Morgan, Nora, and Kevin, were forced to forego some play time when Mom was busy with her manuscript, and for that largesse I thank them. My husband, Jerry, has always been my biggest fan. And sports fan that he is, although it was suggested that I change the name of the section referencing Curtis Flood, I kept it in for him.

Finally, there is an aspect of writing a book that is like giving birth to a baby. First it's just an idea. Then you need to work on it, but you still have nine months or so, which at the beginning seems like a long time. During that time, people are constantly giving you ideas, support, and assistance, but you are the one that needs to sift through those for the most relevant nuggets. When you're down to those last two weeks, suddenly the definition of time changes, and it's hard to think of anything else beyond the impending deadline. Finally the moment of truth arrives, and you are in labor to make this new life happen. The labor can be arduous, emotional, and incredibly strenuous, but somehow you know that ultimately it will be over and you will have his wonderful new baby. Well, I can't wait to deliver this new "baby." I just hope there won't be sleep deprivation to come.

Marion McGovern

PART

I

THE CREST OF
THE WAVE

THE COMPANY
MAN MYTH

"Honey, I'm home." Once a week from 1957 to 1963, Ward Cleaver would come through the kitchen door announcing his arrival from the office. June Cleaver would appear in her starched cotton dress with a string of pearls around her neck and inquire about his day. Then she would go on to tell him about the latest exploits of the Beaver.

Although it seems quaint now, many of us grew up with this image of being a businessperson. Beyond being one of the best television dads of that era, Ward Cleaver was the epitome of the "company man." He'd often work late and stumble home exhausted. He'd be frustrated with company politics and worry about various projects. June was his supportive "corporate wife," joining him at company outings in St. Louis or New York. Unless the show went off the air, we knew Ward would be with that company for the rest of his life. Things surely have changed.

If you transplanted the Cleavers to the present day, chances are that one of them—Ward, or more likely, June—would be a consultant, an independent one, building a practice around an area of expertise and serving clients with a smile. (In June's case, she'd still be wearing those pearls as well.) The big white house in Mayfield would include a home office fully wired to the Internet via DSL. After all, how could you possibly consult in this day and age from bucolic Mayfield unless you were totally online and operating 24 by 7?

Just as *Leave it to Beaver* has disappeared, so too has the concept of the company man, who works throughout his career for one company, climbing the corporate ladder, and finally retiring with a gold watch. The very idea no longer resonates with Americans. The corporate restructuring of the 1970s, followed by subsequent waves of layoffs in the name of reengineering in the 1980s, fundamentally altered the perception of corporate employment.

THE EROSION OF THE EMPLOYEE CONTRACT

Twenty years ago, eager college students actively sought positions with large corporations, such as IBM, GE, or Xerox, because they wanted the assurance of stability for their future career. Like Ward Cleaver, we assumed that once we landed with the right employer, our life would be worked out for us from then on; the paternal corporation would provide opportunities for us to grow and advance, and as long as we did our part, successfully achieving desired corporate goals, then they would do theirs, maintaining our employment status.

Just as eagerly, other entry-level professionals jumped at offers from exciting companies, such as Manufacturer's Hanover Bank (fondly referred to as Manny Hanny), ITEL, or Crown Zellerbach. But these jobs became illustrative of what would befall many workers in corporate America throughout the 1980s, as these positions and their associated future security were eliminated by mergers, bankruptcy, and corporate raiders, respectively.

We need only compare the Fortune 500 in 1980 to the Fortune 500 in 1998 to see how dramatic the change has been. Only 127 companies (24.5 percent) of the 1980 cadre are still on the list. The more telling statistic is that of the 373 that are no longer on the list, many are no longer in existence.

Many people suffered cascading dislocations, surviving merger after merger, as industry consolidations transformed entire economic sectors, such as financial services, telecommunications, and computer hardware. Others opted to jump ship and leave the corporate track, rather than wait for the next inevitable reduction in force, or RIF. New jargon entered the language as downsizing—or better yet, rightsizing—euphemistically replaced layoff as the term of choice to describe this corporate asceticism. Participants, communities, and observers saw this human churn as a sign that the era of the company man was ending.

No longer would the paternalistic corporation afford long-term security for its good performers. Any hope that this trend was reversible was dashed when Hewlett-Packard announced its first-ever employee layoffs in 1991. The venerable computer maker had been a long-term holdout in the downsizing battle, opting to stand by its pledge of lifelong employment; however, rapidly changing technology, global competition, and the realities of the public market forced the company to make a strategic shift.

WORKERS WANT OUT

But the labor market had shifted as well. In the 1970s, professional women began entering the labor market in record numbers. Their ranks increased as a percentage of college graduates and MBA program graduates as well. The resulting two-income couple gave rise to a new demographic segment—the DINCs (double income no children), a target market that electronics, home furnishings, and consumer goods manufacturers courted shamelessly. But then these new professional women aged and became parents.

In 1989, Felice Schwartz, the founder of Catalyst, published the now-famous article, "The Mommy Track." She highlighted to America something it already knew: Women were advancing in the business world, but the intersection of career and family was creating dissonance. More specifically, in professional service firms and corporations, senior-level women who wanted more time for parenting their young children were often shoved off the "fast track" or the "partnership track" and relegated to the "Mommy track."

This subordinate path elevated the glass ceiling for these mothers, and Schwartz's article served as a wake-up call for many people who feared that women would now be effectively precluded from reaching the upper echelons of corporate America. Companies were asked to develop more family-friendly policies. *Working Mother* magazine's list of the best workplaces for women became big news. Some companies created mentorship opportunities for executive women who were also parents to ensure that the Mommy track did not entirely derail a promising career.

The exodus of many women from corporate America was greeted with great concern; however, what many people failed to recognize at the time was that a significant percentage of these women were not leaving the business arena for good. Rather, they were adopting a new business model that would harmonize with the demands of their more complicated family life. They couldn't wait for corporate America to figure out how to create jobs that were congruent with the new reality of the American family; that is, two working parents and a shortage of good childcare. Many companies still had the Ward Cleaver prototype in mind, and these women knew that June Cleaver wasn't at home making dinner anymore.

Other disenfranchised professional groups also emerged. George Bush highlighted one in his 1988 presidential campaign, where he applauded a new spirit of volunteerism in America and gave this movement a name—the "Thousand Points of Light." Many people found this desire for successful professionals to give back to be at odds with the company man notion, because many companies did not empower the employee with the time to pursue such time-intensive altruism. In many businesses—investment banking, consulting, and advertising to name three of the toughest— professionals lived like Bedouins, moving from client site to client site, racking up the frequent flyer miles, and considering their Executive Premier flying status as a badge of honor. This lifestyle left no time for community service, let alone family, and for many workers it was not ultimately sustainable.

Now, the challenge is becoming even more acute as personal service companies have sprung up to service daily household needs. Large professional services firms, understanding that they have effectively taken the home out of "home life," will underwrite payments for someone to come walk employees' dogs, water their plants at home, and even pinch hit for a sick nanny; some employers will do anything to ensure that their team is working constantly. With the new "dot.com" community in the picture, even more unique and creative hiring and retention practices have exploded. But eventually, although the home fires may be burning brightly, the employee will be merely burned out.

So thousands of executives, beginning in the early 1980s and continuing today, created a new professional life as a way to gain control over their time. For some, it was a way to pursue personal passions, community interests, and artistic muses. Historically, it has always been difficult to pursue art for a living. Were it not for the Medici family, Michelangelo may not have had the opportunity to create the masterpieces he did. Similarly, Mozart relied on the beneficence of a patron. Today, such supporters are tough to come by, so the best solution for many artists is to bankroll yourself.

The number of accomplished independent consultants who are actually artists in disguise is inestimable. Just as my sister heeded the words of my mother: "Don't go into art, you'll never make money," so, too, did countless others. The demographic shift toward independent work enabled many of these individuals to reevaluate their life goals. Having subrogated their true artistic passion in the interest of building a lucrative, professional career, they could now use the expertise developed in that career to subsidize their art. In the M^2 consulting network, we have sculptors, playwrights, novelists, musicians, and painters who are now able to advance their artistic gift while still earning a great living.

In 1994, we worked on several projects with an accomplished human resources consultant who was also a truly eloquent communicator. As such, we were not surprised to learn that she was consulting in organizational development in order to have free time and support herself while writing a book about military heroines of World War II. We were pleased to learn three years later that she had secured a publisher for her book.

For other professionals, this new way of life provided a way to pursue ancillary business ideas. Take the example of a senior information technology (IT) consultant who also happened to be a pilot. He consulted because he was launching a business, the detailing of private planes. Apparently, plane owners have no place to take their crafts to be handwashed and spot painted. He thought that such a service in selected regional airfields would be a welcome and highly marketable one.

In true entrepreneurial style, many businesspeople simply realized they could make more money and be more professionally satisfied if they could just set up their own shops. This was especially true for those workers who rose through the ranks of the professional services world, such as management consulting, advertising, public relations, and accounting. Some of them had a different perspective on how they wanted to deliver value. Others just wanted to choose their own clients and engagements. All of them knew that they didn't need a big firm to find or produce quality work. More importantly, they recognized the high cost of overhead.

Professional services firms (accountants, lawyers, etc.) don't set fees on a margin basis but rather on a multiple basis. Most billing rates are set between two and three times annualized salaries, divided by an assumed billable hour figure. As an employee, although your billing rate may be $300 per hour to the client, your salary would more likely be less than $100 per hour. The $200 differential covers overhead, nonbillable time, and profit.

The independent consultant refugee from this world recognizes that his or her billing rate will decrease from the lofty $300-per-hour range because he or she is no longer a branded service—clients pay a premium for the pedigree of the McKinsey methodology or the Booz Allen way. Conversely and more importantly, the overhead portion decreases dramatically, making the net dollars received a significantly higher sum in the independent marketplace.

THE NEW "FREELANCER"

As a result of these factors, a new free agent movement was born and has been heralded in publications such as *Fast Company*, which has become the business digest of choice for this talent segment.

The truth of the matter is that free agents have been around in different business venues for many years. In fact, the term *freelancer* dates back to the Middle Ages, when it was used to describe mercenary knights. A "free" lancer was an available soldier, with lance of course, who could defend a lord for a price. Although some independent consultants today might object to the mercenary characterization, there is a kernel of truth to the analogy. A mercenary, unlike a conscripted soldier, worked for a market price, albeit a very imperfect and largely corrupt market.

Today's free agent is market-driven as well. Companies have come to recognize the effectiveness and efficiency of using independent expertise. Professionals have recognized the benefits of being independent. The market has reached critical mass and continues to grow rapidly, becoming more efficient every day.

Chapter 2

WHY COMPANIES USE INDEPENDENT TALENT

◆ **THE SPEED OF BUSINESS**

All you need to do to appreciate the pace of business today is to reflect on the companies making headlines. eBay, which makes money by staging auctions over the Internet, is a terrific case in point. Put yourself back ten years, and you wouldn't be able to decipher their business proposition, because the Internet in 1990 was still an obscure network known only to academics and scientists. In the relatively short span of a decade, new technologies have spawned ideas that have grown into companies that now, in the case of eBay, have market capitalizations approaching those of blue chip stalwarts such as Ford Motor Company. In fact, in 1998, Digital Equipment Corp. (later acquired by Compaq) paid more for the upstart, profitless search engine Alta Vista than Ford paid for the time-honored, synonymous with safety, extremely profitable Swedish auto manufacturer Volvo.

If you look at language as a harbinger of fundamental societal change, then once again new words have entered the vocabulary—terms like portal, search engine, and browser. For most Americans, the Internet has been adopted faster than any other technological innovation, such as radio, television, or even the home computer. This adoption rate is indicative of the increased pace driving what the marketplace demands of business.

Five-year planning cycles are no longer effective in a world where technology can become obsolete in less than six months. In a global marketplace where the factors of production can differ dramatically across continents, companies must continually control product cost or risk losing share to an offshore producer. For retailers, the risk is no longer that you could lose a customer to the competitor across town; now you need to worry about the e-commerce merchant as well.

This frenetic pace affects most sectors, even those not in technology, because of the corollary cultural shifts occurring in America. As people work at a faster pace, they demand that products and services are available when they have opportunities to use or buy them. The concept of "bankers' hours," in which banks closed early most days to suit themselves, has been replaced by 24-hour online banking, Saturday hours at most locations, and full-service branches in supermarkets.

How can traditional businesses keep up? They can't—not using the old mode. So new ways to tackle the ever-changing set of priorities have to be developed.

PROJECTIZATION

Tom Peters first coined the term *projectization* in his book *Liberation Management*. He cited M^2 as indicative of the trend toward decomposing large initiatives into smaller tasks, ultimately arriving at the series of projects needed to be completed to achieve the result. Initiatives could then be accelerated by considering which projects could occur concurrently rather than sequentially. By definition, the concurrent task project teams presuppose that different people will be handling the work.

Alternatively, projectization could also mean that the same people handled pieces of the work, but intermittently. An expert in one particular field could be called in to consult in that area only when needed, contributing to the team along the way as appropriate.

Let's consider an example: A major California bank needed to be able to meet the needs of its customers for greater access, so in 1995 it decided to co-locate branches in retail outlets convenient to its customers. An agreement was reached with a major retail chain, so the end game became clear: open full-service branches throughout the West in selected grocery store locations.

Developing a whole new distribution channel for any business is not a trivial exercise; add to it the fact that it would be developed with someone else's valuable real estate, and it becomes quite a challenge. The bank created a large project with many subprojects to implement this rather daunting task.

A master project team was created. Key members of the bank staff were adjuncts, but a leader was needed to keep the project going. An outside consultant was secured from M^2 to coordinate all of the various constituencies in the bank who needed to be involved. These factions included the regional branch management, information technology, and the policy and procedures department.

Certain large segments of work were discrete enough to be defined as separate projects. One project in particular—the space-planning portion of how a bank branch could most logically be inserted into a bustling retail location—was outside the realm of normal bank business and embedded expertise. A facilities expert was retained to develop the model for the branch layout and then specify the required furniture and equipment configuration.

An adjunct to this project was the image dimension of the branch, its signage, logo usage, and collateral. A communications consultant was engaged to develop this piece, consistent with prevailing policies in traditional branches. Finally, the technical and operational dimension of the branch in terms of the remote central processing unit (CPU) communication, ATM network linkage, and teller platform technology needed to be coordinated as well.

Meanwhile, the original project manager handled the other necessary components of starting up a branch, leveraging existing resources within the bank to tailor the procedures manuals, operating guidelines, and training programs.

Once the various approaches were created, and deliverables defined, they could be grafted into one framework for how a branch is opened in this type of retail store. With that framework, the bank could then just replicate it in every location it chose.

The projectization approach was effective for the bank because it leveraged its own intellectual capital without adding permanent overhead; the outside team used what the bank knew and made a whole new channel happen, without adding staff. Additionally, bank employees were not overtaxed with the hands-on effort to launch a new initiative, but their critical input was effectively utilized.

A BRAVE NEW WORLD

The breakneck speed of business and the explosion of technology mean that an exponential level of complexity now exists in the marketplace. New products are being introduced at a rate unmatched in our lifetime. An increasing percentage of American companies are doing business internationally. Industries that once competed solely on price or service are now being forced into the realm of e-business.

This barrage of new, competitive pressures and opportunities means that companies must have the skills to address issues competently in unfamiliar areas. Here is a perfect example of this situation: In 1995, M^2 received a call from a South African CEO. Trade sanctions were about to be dropped, and as a result, this industrial textile company now had a worldwide expansion opportunity; however, because no one in South Africa had been able to compete internationally before, the country's workers lacked knowledge about marketing abroad. The CEO knew he had to import expertise into his company in order to develop and execute an international marketing strategy.

M^2 ultimately sent three consultants to South Africa. One expert was charged with developing an export market for the company's core product line of industrial fibers and textiles. Another consultant was charged with exploiting several niche opportunities in the consumer market—a task that he, with M^2's help, recognized required a different skill set. The third team member was responsible for creating an international marketing function, defining the principles, processes, training, and hiring programs necessary to effectively compete globally.

The interesting lesson to learn here is that the emphasis was on building a core competency for the company. Alternatively, sometimes the desire is far more focused on an individual's competencies.

A small but rapidly growing manufacturing concern has been a regular client of M^2 because they want to build the competencies of their employees. The company has always been employee-oriented; for example, it offered English as a second language (ESL) classes gratis at its facility for its largely foreign-born factory staff. More important in terms of potential constraints to its future growth, it always promoted from within wherever possible, which meant that the factory manager was "home grown."

As the little company grew and demand for its product increased, the CEO developed aggressive goals for continued growth; however, achieving these goals meant developing world-class techniques in the factory. This CEO looked to M^2 to provide mentoring to his staff. He didn't want someone to come in and install new manufacturing techniques; rather, he wanted someone to teach his plant manager how to be a world-class manufacturing manager. We found a highly experienced senior manufacturing consultant who had run worldwide operations for Del Monte. He had retired but found retirement boring, so supplementing his leisure time with consulting work, especially with interesting clients, was a wonderful bonus for him. On a part-time basis over the space of several months, he tutored the plant manager in real time, handling projects, issues, and challenges faced by his student.

As an aside, this engagement was profiled in an article in the *Asahi Shinbun*, the Japanese equivalent of the *Wall Street Journal*, in 1995. The interview, in which both the consultant and I participated, was fascinating. The Japanese economics editor found it difficult to comprehend the fact that the consultant did not have an economic motive for doing this work. The consultant's retirement income was healthy, so the intellectual stimulation, not the compensation, motivated him. Moreover, the notion that an individual could be satisfied with less than full-time work also seemed outlandish to the reporter. This was a cultural distinction for sure.

The project was so successful that the CEO subsequently turned to us for similar mentoring roles in sales management and human resources.

NINETY PERCENT OF SUCCESS

Woody Allen once said: "Ninety percent of success is showing up." That's all well and good if you are running the show, as he is, but when a key manager doesn't show up, it can be a big problem for maintaining company momentum.

As such, many companies use consultants as a way to fill in short-term gaps in their management team. Much as business has learned that contract temporaries, whether for the receptionist or the clerk, ensure that productivity doesn't suffer, they have learned that management vacancies can cause problems, too.

Almost 20 years ago, well before my own consulting career began, I once worked in bank operations. As a new analyst, I was tasked with developing the capacity plans for the lockbox unit, the group that processed retail credit payments. The manager understood his operation intimately, making forecasts for the days when most people would submit checks for gas, utility, or department store charges. He also knew when the critical peak periods would be by day, week, and month of the cycle. Using his forecasts, I then arrayed the staffing plan, adjusting full-time equivalent (FTE) levels for vacations, new hires, and other vacancies. We would then fill in with contract labor to ensure that we never had an empty check processing station at a peak time.

Looking back through my lens of M^2, it is fascinating to notice that the vacancies in the management ranks of this company never got similar attention. The bank just ignored six-week and twelve-week voids among its upper ranks. This situation suggests that the company had more management staff than it needed, so it could stretch for even as long as three months if it had to accommodate a vacancy. Perhaps it hadn't structured the organization in a way that required continued contributions by its management team. Either way, it points to an organizational dysfunction. Not unsurprisingly, that bank was merged out of existence in the mid-1980s.

M^2 itself may be the best example of creative use of consulting expertise to fill management voids. We aggressively staff a "bench" for our client services function. Our Client Services Managers, or CSMs, make the matches between our consultants and clients. They have a tremendously time-sensitive job; any failure on our part to ensure that we have enough CSMs means that our service level may be slow.

On an ongoing basis, we identify two to three former search, recruiting, or staffing consultants who have what we would look for in a CSM. At our expense, we train them for a few days and then we say goodbye, with the understanding that we may call them at any time to ask them to come in and help us through a tough time. In the case of extended vacations or sabbaticals, we will know in advance and contract with them for coverage. In some cases, such as an unexpected illness or a tremendous boost in business volumes, we may need emergency assistance. The latter situation is why we always make sure that we have a few people on the bench, because good people are often busy or unavailable, and we need to be sure that we fill open slots quickly.

The acquisition environment is another key area for interim talent. The acquirer often needs to understand better what capabilities may be resident in the acquired team and is therefore reluctant to hire full-time employees. In the meantime, work must be done, so project-based consultants are the perfect answer. In the acquired entity, many of the best senior managers depart quickly, preferring to be in charge of their own professional destinies rather than wait to see whether they survive the inevitable management purge. As such, keeping initiatives going in this transitional period can be difficult without additional expertise on board.

AGENTS OF CHANGE OR STABILITY

Even in this ever-changing global arena, companies can hit plateaus. Certain things work, we stick to them, and we don't think to ask why we are still doing it the same way. Similarly, we can run out of ideas, or worse yet, begin revisiting old ideas we never liked in the first place. If you are in a rut, then you need to do something to get out of it, and a fresh perspective is often just the ticket. Consultants who have an entirely different frame of reference on your business, challenge, or opportunity may be able to drive the organization to a new view of the marketplace.

This is especially true of industries that are undergoing deregulation. We have had clients specifically request consultants with expertise in wildly competitive free-market arenas as a way to percolate fresh thinking through a staid organization.

Similarly, an outsider can be best when internal politics create problems and render some issues too hot to handle. In some companies, difficult issues are ignored because no one wants to open Pandora's box. An unbiased observer is often the best person to open that box. A consultant can be perceived as unaligned and, therefore, more objective in his or her assessment of the issue.

> Being an outsider is much more of an advantage than a disadvantage. You are brought in because the client lacks your expertise. You must quickly and adroitly "read" the culture and power structure of your client organization to anticipate barriers. Projecting an attitude, which doesn't purport to know it all—but rather knows the right questions to ask— usually helps to break down resistance and generate acceptance. Worst case, as an outsider, I can walk away with minimal baggage if the situation becomes intolerable—not as easy if you are an employee. —*David Potter*

See Appendix for a short profile of each consultant quoted.

In one situation, M^2 was asked to intervene in the case of an international microfiber producer with a poorly performing division. Tensions were high internally about what course of action could be pursued, so an outside expert was brought in to evaluate the business potential for this faltering division. The consultant was able to objectively determine that the business model being pursued by the firm around this particular product line was not sufficiently robust to yield the type of pretax returns enjoyed by the rest of the operating units. On the other hand, he was also able to independently value the underlying technology and present a strategy to the company's board to sell off the line to a company in a completely different business that would utilize it for a completely different application.

Again, the changing world order of Internet time had added an inverse corollary to the change agent—the need for a stability agent. As a dot.com company grows faster and faster, needing increasingly more people more quickly, it is being forced to adopt the practices of a big company. In essence, it is growing into the need for infrastructure processes (that is, hiring and firing guidelines, financial systems, and employee benefits) before its management team is ready to tackle these areas.

As such, the dot.com is forced to bring in an expert to develop a recruiting process for them, to create a methodology in an otherwise chaotic world. In many cases, our consultants are the most senior members of the team of some of our Internet clients, and their business maturity and expertise provides invaluable assistance to these high-growth companies.

The truth of the matter is that with some of our hotshot start-ups, we need to bring in a "mom." One of our senior human resources executives needed to explain to our client's dynamic management team that basketballs could not be hurled at employees, even in frustration. The fact that such an observation needed to be made shows just how naïve some of the new economy entrepreneurs can be; like an adolescent needing a parent to set limits even though those limits may be unwelcome at times, these new companies need some parental influence as well.

As *The Industry Standard* reported:

> At a time when easy money and fast growth are covering a multitude of sins among Web starts, old rules rule the new economy. I'll gladly concede new rules of business, such as the power of increasing returns or the deconstruction (and reconstruction) of intermediation. Yet most startups still get tripped up by failing to cover such basics as matching the right finance to the business model, hiring and managing the right people, and learning how to learn and adapt.—*Tom Ehrenfeld*, in "Just

Managing—The Old Rules that Rule the New Economy," February 28, 2000

Consultants who specialize in this area (that is, working with start-ups or venture-backed enterprises) bring a special sort of care to their stability agent role. They have the wisdom gained from their collective experiences that enable them to assume an implicit leadership role.

> I have never felt like an "outsider" because I have always felt, due to my experience, that I am an evangelist and it is my duty to be included. I take the approach that it is my responsibility to go through discovery with every employee, be it receptionist or CEO, and that my duty is to gain trust, be ethical, truthful, and always on the team. I sign up for whatever it takes. —*Sandy Di Nubilo*

WHY INDIVIDUALS CHOOSE FREE AGENCY

chapter 3

CURTIS FLOOD WAS NOT ALONE

When he refused to be traded to Cleveland, Curtis Flood fundamentally changed major league baseball and ultimately all professional sports forever. His desire to be able to control some of the key aspects of his career once he had become a recognized professional seemed to him to be an inalienable right. Interestingly, Flood was not a major star or even a wildly popular player; he was just a good, solid performer who thought the power wielded by the owners was beyond the pale.

The parallel is there for many free-agent businesspeople as well. When we ask our consultants why they decide to hang out a shingle and go into business for themselves, the overwhelming desire is for control.

> During the last 30 years, there have been numerous times when I have entertained the notion of taking a real job—usually instigated by a satisfied client. I'd be lying if I said I didn't care about the intellectual stimulus that comes with an ongoing association with other professionals, the synergism, and yes, even the potential for steady financial growth. But these rare moments always seem to pass by quickly— usually as fast as it takes me to close my next consulting contract. Freedom always seems to win me over—I guess I have a true passion for doing my own thing. —*Barry Deutsch*

Whether it is control over where they work, like Curtis, their hours, or their vacations, overwhelmingly, it is a desire to make work fit into their lives and not vice versa. One of our consultants of Dutch descent explained that she became an independent practitioner because she thought that American vacation structures were untenable; being used to at least six weeks of vacation annually, she couldn't continue in the American mode of two weeks per year.

Control can be lost in insidious ways in a large organization. Losing control of your own career is a fate that many workers endure in the ranks of the Fortune 1000. One consultant related a tale of betrayal in a management change.

> My boss soon became my mentor . . . . For four years, my skills blossomed and I felt very confident and capable at my current position. I was respected by my peers and truly exceeded my boss's daily expectations. Four years into my

> tenure, my mentor left the company to take a better opportunity . . . . So, the new vice president of marketing came on board, and here I was again left to prove myself and my abilities. Well, I was told by my current boss that she had to "pick her battles," and my impending promotion was not a battle she wanted to take on. I was crushed! I had worked so hard only to have this stranger decide my destiny and tell me that my efforts will only give me a pat on the back, not the promotion I so deserved . . . . I now decide my destiny! Success is decided by me! —*Stephanie Carhee*

In today's 24-by-7 world, time has a currency all its own. Control over one's time was a key issue cited by many consultants.

WHO, WHAT, WHEN, AND WHERE

The desire for control is really a catchall motivation that has a journalistic dimension—that is, a who, what, when, and where. The "who" encompasses defining for yourself who you want to have as clients. This may mean avoiding industries that are not appealing, like weapons or tobacco. Alternatively, it may mean appealing to a certain segment. Many consultants with blue chip corporate backgrounds enter consulting to the not-for-profit world because they now want control over whom they serve. Finally, it can be the specifics of whom one works with on a day-to-day basis.

> Rather than concerning myself with the idiosyncrasies of the leader of one organization, I am challenged to understand and deal with the idiosyncrasies of all leaders and managers. Rather than being forced to deal with one leader, I can choose not to deal with any of those that may not be a good fit. I am confident that the future is in my control—not the control of an owner who "owns" me. —*Dana Free*

Some consultants want control over what they do, a sphere of influence that as a mere mortal in a large enterprise was beyond their reach. At M^2, we see this often with the alumni from large consulting firms. Exposed to many types of industries and projects, they may have been able to identify the type of work they most enjoyed, but they may not have had the opportunity to do it again. For these individuals, the type of work—the "what"—is most critical.

> I became an independent consultant because I reached a point in my consulting career, after working for four large consulting firms, where I felt I was in the best position to control my own destiny. I wanted to manage my client relationships more directly rather than having to comply with policies and practices established by my consulting firm employers. I also wanted greater control over my schedule and the ability to work more from my home office. For example, I wanted to be able to take time off between projects without an employer breathing down my neck about the next billable project. —*Janet Birgenheimer*

Another freelance human resources organizational development (OD) consultant had been with a large benefits consulting firm. She had conducted several cultural assessment audits with clients, evaluating the nature of the company culture, how it was perceived by employees, and how it supported or frustrated company goals. The firm then repositioned itself more in the compensation field, making the OD dimension of projects less of a priority. This strategic shift prompted her to set up her own business because the cultural assessments were the most exciting and fulfilling aspects of the job.

The "when" variable is a control issue for several kinds of consultants, the largest segment being parents. Many consultants today chose this lifestyle in order to have control over their time and recalibrate their schedule to spend more free time with their families. Whether it is the new mother, the parent coaching the soccer team, or the adult child of aging ill parents, time for family has become a more valued commodity in this day and age.

> I think almost anything we do that's important to us comes down to time and money. Here's what I mean. Sometimes I kid myself and say I love consulting, but the work is really no different than when I had a job. I just get paid three to four times what I was paid as an employee and work less hours now. I spent 12 years in the corporate world, made a six-figure income, and thought I was doing well. Promotions and titles have an insidious way of making one feel successful. For me it comes down to money and time. Or maybe I just love my wife and daughter too much to have a job. You've probably heard it before; here's how children spell love—T-I-M-E. —*Lynn Astalos*

Thinking back to the Cleaver family, Ward Cleaver never had to worry about family matters because June was clearly home and able to handle any emergency. Now fast forward to today—with both of the Cleavers working, both will most likely demand family time to ensure that Wally and the Beaver get the attention they need when they need it.

The "when" can also be the motive for those who have interesting and time-consuming avocations. One accomplished M^2 consultant is also an avid surfer. As any surfer will tell you, the waves aren't always great, but when they are totally awesome, the real surfers come out of the woodwork. In this particular consultant's case, client work must sometimes be suspended if it's that time of year when the waves curl. As such, his career needed to support a lifestyle that was free to be in sync with the ocean currents.

> I also wanted freedom from a day-to-day routine that had me reporting to the same place each day at the same time. I wanted more flexibility in taking time off during the week as well as how much vacation time I took. In the 11 years I have been on my own, there have been several times

I have thought of returning to a full-time job, but I never seriously considered it except in the first few years I was out on my own. The main reasons were the ups and downs of income, the uncertainty of cash flow, continuous marketing, which is my least favorite activity, fear of not keeping up with technology and business trends, and not seeing the long-term effect of my work; however, my desire for freedom both in time and work have always strongly over-ridden any real move to find an internal position. —*Carole Rehbock*

Control over where you worked was what drove Curtis Flood. (With all due respect to the people of Cleveland, he did have a point.) It also plagues double-income couples, who follow the career-development trajectory of one partner to new locales. Often, the following partner pursues a consulting path.

Alternatively, corporate moves may prompt people to become independent consultants. The San Francisco Bay area has an enormous supply of indigenous consulting expertise for the simple reason that people like the city by the Bay. Asked to move to Texas following the SBC Communications merger, many employees said "no," and several of those people became consultants. Similarly, many financial services experts made the consultant career choice when Bank of America was bought by a North Carolina suitor and many key roles were moved to the Southeast.

REASONS OUTSIDE OF YOUR CONTROL

I became an independent consultant as a result of a major restructuring at a high-tech company at which I worked. My departure was a result of political maneuvering. My performance was outstanding on the job, as evidenced by excellent reviews, very large bonuses, and very large salary increases. So I decided that this was going to be the last time

> that I would experience negative reward for a
> job well done. It dawned on me that I had more
> of my best interests at heart than did any
> employer. As such I took control of my career
> and my time. —*David Ellison*

Although most of the consultants with whom M^2 works made the decision by choice, many people join the ranks of free agency by default via corporate restructuring or job elimi-nations. Outplacement firms and career development en-tities work with the senior partners of the newly unemployed to discuss independent consulting as an option. Many former managers gravitate to it quickly, preferring the results-oriented consulting or interim management environment to a prior corporate lethargy.

> I became an independent consultant during the
> summer of 1991 when my job as director of
> telecommunications (the first in the company)
> for Seagate Technology was eliminated along
> with 2,000 other jobs. Seagate had lost $80
> million that quarter and could not run a loss for
> another quarter and survive. Most of the
> objectives of the job that I filled had also been
> met. I have subsequently found I prefer being
> an independent consultant because of the
> diversity of assignments and the flexibility it
> provides in one's personal life. —*William Meyer*

Interestingly, this is the primary reason why individuals make this career choice in the United Kingdom. The pre-cursor to this book, *Interim Management*, describes this business niche in the United Kingdom, where the inde-pendent talent marketplace is clearly different. The indi-viduals choosing the interim management route are somewhat homogeneous—they are men in their late forties with a minimum of 15 to 20 years of line experience in a UK corporation. There is even a disclaimer about not including women in this book about interim management, because the population of this demographic segment of interims includes so few women.

> Mentioning ladies reminds me of the problem of gender. At a recent count 96 percent of the agency's portfolio was male and 4 female— which approximates closely to the proportion amongst U.K. senior management. This proportion is changing as the younger generation of managers comes through, but in the meantime it seemed convenient to write this book as if all were male. —*Dennis Russell,* in *Interim Management*, p. xiv.

Similarly, M² has an affiliated company in South Africa, Axis Interim Management. Its array of expertise is far more similar to the UK model than it is to our U.S. one. In fact, many of the interim managers used by Axis on projects in South Africa are British expatriates.

One could argue that this difference may be more culturally than geographically derived. The entrepreneurial spirit of people choosing their own destiny as illustrated by the prior section may be peculiar to Americans. Research shows that companies are started more frequently in the United States than in any other developed or developing country. Setting up a consulting practice is analogous to starting a company. As such, perhaps the same cultural norms and attributes that make Americans more likely to start a company also make them more likely to be free agents.

> Flexibility was my main motivation to become an independent consultant. I wanted to set my own time as well as to decide which projects I wanted to work on. On top of that, I wanted to see how I would do as an entrepreneur, dealing with the up and downs (uncertainty) of running a business. —*Jolanda de Boer*

As the projectization trend becomes more global, it will be interesting to see where the free-agent populations thrive and where they do not. Although entrepreneurial empathy may be cultural, infrastructure is national. Health insurance, taxes, employment laws, and other local factors may impact the growth of the free-agent population internationally. Any of these factors could negate one of the vectors of control.

Conversely, as the world becomes more global, distances shrink. The U.S. free agents will invariably become more mobile, and other countries will be exposed to the vibrant U.S. ethos for an independent career and lifestyle. It is happening already.

> Freedom is the payoff. If I had stayed in the corporate life, then I would not have had the opportunity to do many of the things that I have done. I taught overseas for two years. I could do this as I finished an assignment and then just left for two years. Living overseas was a great experience for me. I also found that I liked teaching and have taught part time since I returned. I had known that one of the things I liked as a consultant was that I was usually training people and that training and teaching are very similar, if not identical. —*Paul Thode*

Chapter 4

"MIND SETS" AS WELL AS SKILL SETS

Ever-increasing numbers of individuals are opting out of traditional employer–employee relationships, sustained by a simultaneous evolution of more virtual working arrangements. As technology has reinvented the infrastructure of most corporations across the board, demand for the highly skilled knowledge worker has placed a premium on portable intellectual capital, which can be added (and then dropped) by an organization on an as-needed basis. This "dropping and adding" bears little resemblance to its previous incarnation in the old economic paradigm, in which the rhythm of staffing up and cutting back created initial demands for the services of contingent workers. It is instead more reflective of the drive of companies today to be fueling growth with the newest, freshest, and most expedient get-to-market strategies, provided by the knowledge worker.

In the old economic paradigm, individuals in the management ranks often held positions that were highly "custodial" in nature. They were overseers of people, processes, and problems for which they had neither personal ownership, nor any meaningful rubric by which to measure success at the end of the day (week, month, year, etc.). The extraordinary sense of urgency that characterizes the new economy has created a divergent niche for specific, "deliverable-driven" work parcels that are both fed and encouraged by the willingness and high skill level of available talent.

Independent consultants who market themselves to these opportunities are those who derive a profound sense of achievement and professional esteem from these latter situations in which specific goals are established, but paths to the realization of these goals are often less finite. The consultant often works alone to map the course; explore possible solutions; devise the strategy; establish the plan, budget, and timeline for accomplishing the task; and then frequently, setting about implementing these concepts. At other times, a team may be participating on the project, but it is a group inspired by a shared sense of purpose and goal orientation. There is ownership of the process and product from beginning to end, as opposed to the kind of "custodial" work their previous lives as corporate managers most frequently offered.

At the 10,000-foot level, this convergence of new attitudes about leveraging intellectual capital from outside an organization to achieve high consequence and high-priority objectives, and this ambition of certain individuals seeking more satisfying work, consequently prods the widespread acceptance of a more virtual workplace.

Bill Meyer, of Menlo Park, California, is in many ways a classic example of these principles. A seasoned professional in the telecommunications field, Bill—like so many layers of management in the downsizing of the early 1990s—found himself squeezed from his regular, full-time role and began rethinking his career path. His professional focus in engineering and operations in the telecommunications world prepared him well for project-based initiatives. He liked the defined beginning, process, and completion of this type of work, and he was able to effectively market himself to a variety of situations.

He found that he was highly stimulated by the diversity of assignments he was able to secure and flexibility that the work afforded. He believes his success over the last decade has been attributed to his ability to clearly understand his own areas of competence and stay within those parameters. In so doing, he takes on only assignments in which his highest degree of expertise can be best showcased. He is committed to being objective, factual, conscientious, and positive when working with clients, and to avoid what he terms the "technical sparring match" with the insiders, which is always a losing proposition.

At the grassroots level, a comprehensive cultural shift is occurring parallel to these transformations in the corporate sphere. The desire and demand for greater control of one's professional and personal satisfaction are often articulated by mid- to senior-level professionals in every industry and within every functional area of expertise. Thinking in terms of the human hierarchy of needs, it is logical that the more technologically advanced, complex, and sophisticated a culture becomes, the more attention to such personal desires its members are likely to demonstrate. The independent consultant population provides consistent data that people are spending more of their energy on the "selves" that exist beyond the perimeter of their eight-to-six identity, and having the ability to sway the logistics of these endeavors is critical to their locus of personal control.

Often, familial considerations prompt members of the higher tiers of management to opt out of their regular corporate servitude. Widespread concerns over the quality, convenience, and economic feasibility of childcare that can be obtained outside of the family structure, as well as increasing esteem placed on the stay-at-home parent, has made the adoption of free-agent status an ever more viable choice. Many parents—women and men alike—share the feeling that they wish to be the primary influences in their children's development, and consequently seek flexibility in days and hours worked (including a cap on the hours per week their roles in reality will imply) and part-time or job-sharing accommodations. As employers struggle simultaneously to attract and sustain the highest caliber of talent in their markets, flexibility of this nature becomes a buzzword in recruiting and retention strategies. Independent management consulting, from both the company in need of talent and the talent in search of the right situation perspectives, is a clear resource.

Hazel Payne, of Berkeley, California, became an independent consultant when she adopted a child. Like Bill, Hazel's corporate experience and portable skill sets made the evolution to a consultant a natural one: Her area of specialization—compensation analysis—lends itself easily to consulting work. The demand for consultants in this arena is fairly consistent; companies often need an objective outsider to evaluate existing incentive structures and other related issues.

For Hazel, as is universally the case for parents of young children, everything is about time. She makes a regular effort to inventory this most precious commodity, tracking tasks for weeks to see which three to five activities consume the greatest portion of her time budget, while still leaving enough room for the personal downtime necessary to recharge. In her planning of work and life, she is also sure to always factor in enough emergency leeway. Among the lessons learned from having an infant is the dictum that no matter how organized and in control rational adults may be, many variables slip outside of these careful parameters, and more often than not the unexpected always flies to the very top of the priority list.

This seasoned rationalism extends to her views on income as well. The oft-repeated quip among independents is that:

"Consulting is great work, when you can get it." Income potential is certainly high but is also relative to how much of one's self and life one is willing to devote to its pursuit. Hazel has adopted a Zen-like attitude about this aspect of her working life; as she puts it, "While an annual income of six figures is one of my goals as a consultant, I am also learning the fine art of reining in my workaholic tendencies and practicing 'enough.'" Like so many high-income-potential professionals who have chosen a similar path as independents, the recognition and importance of that which money cannot buy takes on ever-greater currency. Hazel knows she would not be able to purchase back at some later point in the future these early years in her daughter's life, nor the sanity she relies on to navigate the waters of professional balance.

In addition to family care issues such as these, we often witness individuals with a high degree of commitment to personal interests, which can include ongoing education in fields not specifically related to the daytime identity, hobbies, and community service commitments. In recent years, M^2 has made the acquaintance of a host of such individuals, whose after-hours pursuits included training for marathons, building and funding a women's shelter, playing in bands, and classic car collection and refurbishing. For each of these people, maintaining a high degree of professional esteem and integrity is essential, and the independent consulting lifestyle enables them to do exactly that while not costing them these critical vehicles of self-expression.

Dale Uptegrove, also of Berkeley, California, personifies these tendencies. He is an avid windsurfer in the spring and summer months, an avocation that requires the ability to, as he puts it, "be in the water by 4 p.m." This would have been impossible for Dale as a manager of a staff—with the obligation to clock hours shepherding other people, politics, and miscellaneous tasks, and maintaining the visibility required of a senior-level manager—but is viable for him as a free agent accountable to his productivity and deliverables alone.

For Dale, hourly billing is the reliable index by which his contribution can best be measured. He has expressed amazement over the amount of unproductive time he has witnessed among corporate insiders. He likes how "clean" it is that on those afternoons he finds himself watching the wind blow outside, he can with integrity end his commitment for the day by going off the clock. He sees an enormous advantage for the clients who employ him as well. He is a much more cost-effective contributor, forcing no one to pay for the unproductive hours that seem to be endemic to the traditional employer–employee relationship. In exchange for this enhanced control over his day, he does not require payment for the endless barrage of "team building meetings, mandatory corporate sponsorship meetings, benefits/policy meetings, etc., not that they aren't good things in the abstract, but my life is infinitely richer, simpler, and more productive for not having to go to them." Dale, a specialist in the area of mergers and acquisitions, has learned to market his skills and perspective strategically. Prospective clients can easily grasp the value proposition his services represent.

Dan Kleinman has carved out an enviable lifestyle as well. His consulting practice allows him to leverage his executive-level skills in the design and implementation of total compen-sation plans, the creation of executive pay and special retention packages, the creation of rubrics for performance management structures and processes, and the execution of staff analysis, organizational restructuring, and strategic planning. His deep and broad experience in the banking industry provided him with, as he puts it,

> . . . ample opportunity to be a classic staffer. I was reasonably good at reading the political climate around me and creatively making greedy executives feel less guilty about the excesses they were being accorded, (which made for) a great feeling of self-worth.

Not one to suffer this climate indefinitely, Dan now occupies the time he better controls through consulting by writing murder mysteries, volunteering for Foodrunner (making deliveries of contributions from restaurants and bakeries to shelters, senior centers, etc.), and championing the culinary cause at home. In a blind taste test against his corporate counterparts from Crocker Bank, Wells Fargo, and their kin, Dan's stuffed (wild grains and prunes), boned capon and gumbo offerings surely would best the contributions of these harried, drive-through-breakfast types. And lest we forget to mention, marinades, sauces, and soups also factor highly in his repertoire.

One of the challenges independent consultants face in today's talent-strapped market is to actually defend their independent status with the client companies they serve. It is a highly regular occurrence that free agents are wooed by attractive offers to "come back inside," which further demonstrates the caliber of people making this lifestyle choice. As Hazel Payne remarked: "There have been quite a few times in the last 22 months when I considered going back to regular employment. In today's job market, the regular jobs are plenty, and some of them come with offers that are mighty tempting for a mom with a family to support."

An interesting byproduct of the very presence of highly desirable resources in the shape of management consultants is the way in which companies have been prodded along the progressive-thinking continuum, which has impacted the structure of work itself and benefit plans conceived for regular employees as well.

Client companies, once so easily positioned on the "buy side" with offers of regular, full-time employment, are now hard pressed to counter and must continue to expand their thinking about how to access this valuable demographic. Brokers like M^2 not only help the consultants find suitable projects, but they also take an educational stance with clients. They share success stories and perspectives on "how to think about using an 'X' kind of expert" on a limited basis to achieve their goals the way they once conceived of adding regular, full-time staff to chase growth.

A counterpoint to this urgency for human resources, however, is the amount of initiative and responsibility consultants face in the marketing of their individual "brand" and services. Demand for intellectual capital may be high, but the independent consultant must contend with the relative obscurity he or she will inherit when no longer bound to a traditional corporate patrimony. Whenever consultants are asked what advice they might give to others considering this option, they repeatedly cite the need for creativity, willingness, and perseverance in fostering client relationships.

Bill Meyer's personal recommendation is to "market, market, market," which for him includes development of collateral materials that clearly state his expertise and value proposition, and consistently farming feedback from clients for whom he has worked. To make it simple, he requests three or four sentences that can summarize what he brought to the table on a given assignment and then uses this input in his outreach to prospects. He also aligns himself with as many brokers and Web-enabled resources that could position him appropriately; the more activity he generates, the more exclusive he can be about the work he undertakes.

As these brief case studies illustrate, the motives of those who choose independent management consulting as a career option are always a mixture of the need for a particular professional stimuli and more personal motives. Taken in sum, they reflect a growing cultural shift to work and workplace relationships that demand the exercise of top-drawer skill, intellect, and experience and that offer in exchange the freedom and flexibility to maintain family priorities and/or to pursue self-expressive lives. The independent management consultants and the brokers engaged in market-making on behalf of this population enjoy this privileged moment in history in which work and life may be brought into an harmonious balance without sacrifice of corporate productivity or participation.

PART

II

CREATING YOUR
BRAND OF
EXPERTISE

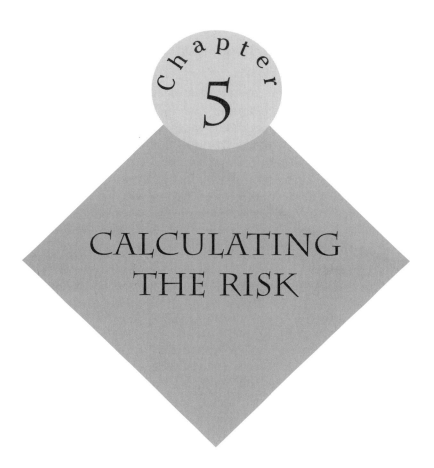

Chapter 5

CALCULATING THE RISK

For many professionals, the decision to go into business as an independent consultant is a challenging one; the prospect of income security and potential wealth growth must be compared against an independent lifestyle and absolute accountability.

The distinction between some of the most frequently asked questions tends to blur when looked at over the long run. Traditional employment offers guaranteed income, but only in the near term. In the long term, the vicissitudes of the business environment guarantee directional shifts, restructuring, and potentially layoffs as well.

Employers provide some modicum of structure to the work, not to mention ancillary benefits such as health insurance and paid vacations. Alternatively, many consultants are able to access traditional benefits through a spousal plan and or the COBRA (Consolidated Omnibus Budget Reconciliation Act) programs of prior employers. In the booming economy of the dot.com world, regular employment with the perks of incentive stock options can offer the promise of quick wealth potential. Consultants can often access such programs, depending on the specific restrictions in the option plan, but we'll explore more on that topic later. Net/net the contrast of traditional employment and consulting may not be so stark.

> The terms of the employment contract are not so important as in the past. An employee can be dropped as easily as a consultant can. For example, when a merger takes place, a market changes, or automation replaces the function. An employee or a consultant pushes more black to the bottom, or their contract is in question. Even today, the consultant is more commonly expected to make a measurable contribution, or hit the road. —*Dana Free*

Similarly, many of the paternalistic services previously provided to the company man are no longer cavalierly dispensed. Employees are increasingly taking a more active role in the management of their benefits programs and the self-education involved. Employees must learn about their 401K options, for example. More and more benefits are being constructed as portable to be able to stay with the employee rather than the employer.

In both cases, project management skills are paramount. For many people, understanding what they can do in the marketplace is reason enough to move, because in the long run, the difference between employment and consulting is negligible.

> In some ways, being an independent contractor has more security. If you define your practice terrain to encompass a variety of industries and experiences, you are creating a more versatile and practical long-term foundation for the "certain uncertainties" of the future. Forgoing hefty employee benefits package can be a hardship if you have a family, but the tradeoff to be weighed is short-term sacrifice versus long-term opportunity. —*David Potter*

Timing is also an issue to consider: In some cases, employers may provide opportunities to build intellectual capital; that is, exposure to training programs and/or thought leadership, which can result in unique experiences that would increase the marketability of a skill set. Alternatively, new client projects regularly present opportunities for skill building as well.

Financing the transition is also important. You and your family must live and eat while the business is building. An accumulated nest egg is a key consideration.

> Independent consulting has a very inconsistent income stream. I did not believe it when others told me that it was necessary to have six to nine *months* worth of money in the bank to live off of during slack times. I now believe. That is a minimum amount of working capital. Three times in the first five years of independent consulting, I had to draw down this account almost to the bottom. Part of it is the slack time, and part of it is getting the cash flow started again. But the family still wanted to eat, and the bank still wanted the mortgage payments; however, I had put the money away, so we weathered the period without having to cut back much on lifestyle. —*Jim White*

The first step in considering the financial aspect is the development of a survival budget. You must examine your domestic financial and personal needs and priorities systematically. Construct it like Maslow's Needs Hierarchy, starting with the most essential requirements first, such as food, shelter, and clothing. Then move on to consider important things, such as school tuition, car payments, and telephone bills. Desirables would be on the next rung, such as vacations, presents, and entertainment expenditures.

Many people are leery to construct such a tiered budget because they are worried about the outcome, but most are often pleasantly surprised to discover that their required survival income may be modest, especially when it may be augmented with other sources of income as well.

A corollary to this is also considering the impact of such a move on your family. From the day that you open your home office, you have also dramatically changed your domestic partner's life. From seeing you 20 percent of the time in a good week, they may now see you much more, especially if they do not work outside of the home. Children may be so thrilled to have you home that it may be difficult to disengage from the home portion of the home office.

Certainly, parents should not make the assumption that by having a home office, childcare expenditures can be reduced. You will still need childcare for any of the period during which you intend to work. In fact, make sure that expense is rooted firmly in your survival budget. When I started the company, I had focus groups with consultants, and one pregnant young consultant suggested that she would work when the baby slept. I gave her the benefit of the doubt because this was her first child and she obviously had no idea what she was getting into as a new parent. Nor did she understand that eventually, the child would not be sleeping nearly as much. Bottom line, both work and family deserve focused attention, so don't give both short shrift.

Similarly, quite apart from the disruption in lifestyle, your family and friends will have anxieties and concerns for you and your future. You need to share your excitement about this new direction and your confidence that consulting work will materialize. You must also acknowledge honestly any concerns you have or any parameters you have set on the effort. For example, if you plan to give it a try for six months and see how you do, then be sure to explain that to your husband or wife as well.

Along the same lines, consider your health, too. If you have any area of weak health, then the transition to an independent lifestyle could have both a beneficial as well as a baneful impact. Heart conditions, ulcers, and high blood pressure may have been controllable as an employee, but the stress of worrying about your own income security may aggravate these conditions. Alternatively, the freedom to plan your own day, exercise, and attend any required medical regimen regularly may offset these concerns.

Perhaps the biggest factor in the decision then is the bottom line—the fear in the recognition that the success of your own consulting practice depends on only one thing—your own performance. This last factor alone often paralyzes people into remaining in the traditional world of work.

> Perpetuating an income stream is obviously very important, and generally, it is easier to do so as an employee. As a professional consultant, you have to continually reinvent and remake yourself professionally. You have to continue to remarket yourself. It takes more effort as a consultant to acquire and sustain an income stream. Intellectually, we consultants are attentive to securing the next engagement; emotionally, we enjoy the times between engagements. It is a perk, but not for one of timid nature. —*David Ellison*

So, for those who are contemplating the decision of starting Independent Consulting Incorporated, here are three key questions to ask yourself before you even think twice about it.

1. Do you really have an expertise companies will buy?
2. Do you work well independently or potentially in isolation?

3. Can you tell a client that his or her strategy, approach, or plan is wrong?

If all of the answers are "yes," then work on a personal business plan is warranted. If any of your answers are negative, then don't quit your day job quite yet.

QUESTION ONE: MARKETABILITY

> One should never attempt consulting without expert knowledge and experience that demonstrates and supports the claim of expert knowledge. People between jobs make the worst consultants. The prerequisite skills for professional consulting are rarely found in job seekers. —*David Ellison*

No one wants a mediocre expert. If your skills aren't strong enough to claim mastery, then read no further. Any question about the marketability of your expertise will impact your potential earning power. Assuming you have a marketable talent, the question then is how much do you need to make annually, and by extension, is there enough of a market for your intellectual capital to support that income level.

> The biggest lesson has to be commitment—to never stop growing in my specialty area (organization development)—a continuous commitment to being focused, positive, and self-motivated—a total commitment to accepting, and even enjoying, the hard reality of life that no matter how good business is currently, you're never more than six months away from bankruptcy. —*Barry Deutsch*

If you are independently wealthy and consulting is an avocation rather than the primary means of lifestyle support, then pursuing an independent practice may still be a viable option. Many consultants with whom we have worked over the years are senior managers who have opted to take early retirement. For them, consulting is not an income imperative so much as it is a way to remain intellectually stimulated.

For most people, though, concerns about the marketability of the expertise should prompt a research effort. Internet job sites can make this research much easier. Sites positing projects like bizbuyer.com, envia.com, or freeagent.com can quickly give you an indication of the demand for your skill set. A note of caution, however: the Internet can suggest feast or famine.

On the feast side, you may find that every other project listing on one site or another is something that is right up your alley. That is a great endorsement that your skills are in demand, but don't get overconfident and assume that you can just set up shop by virtue of the business that is out there on the Internet. Many of these sites have lots of shoppers and far fewer buyers. For some, the fill rate—that is, the proportion of projects that are actually filled by people responding to the e-mail posting—is in the single digits. The low fill rate doesn't imply that the skill set is not in demand; it just suggests that you will need multiple marketing channels, not just the Internet sites, to sell your services.

On the other end of the spectrum, you may find nothing that seems to be your style in these listings. Don't give up hope, though, because you can still assess your marketability offline. Invite some trusted colleagues to lunch together or serially to discuss the option with them, but be sure to choose someone who would be a likely client. Try to ascertain from them what type of work they would offer you were you a consultant and at what rate. If they hesitate, explore the reasons behind their concerns.

Value-added brokers like M^2 can also be a source of input about the marketability of your skills. Keep in mind that these interim management firms are not in the business of career counseling advice; however, they are always looking for new talent. You should be able to tell from the way they handle your query how interesting and, therefore, saleable, your background is to them.

The best firms interview consultants before presenting them to clients. Find out if the firm you are contacting does interviews and, if so, push for a proactive interview. Alternatively, probe to see if your profile would have been a fit for any of the engagements they completed in the last six months. Be prepared for them to be noncommittal, and do not take it as a negative. If they respond affirmatively, however, that can certainly be seen as a positive.

◈ QUESTION TWO: THE TAO OF CONSULTING

Many Eastern religions recognize the wise solitary holy man/person living an ascetic life and growing in wisdom. In Buddhism these revered figures abide by the Tao, which is a way to live harmoniously according to a set of rules. Independent consulting has its own Tao, which is decidedly in contrast to traditional employment, and this aspect of consulting can be difficult for rookies to master.

Most of us began our careers in organizations peopled by all sorts of characters: the workaholic, the party animal, the technical wizard, the ambitious opportunist, the compassionate leader, and so forth. Within this often motley crew of college students, MBAs, new hires, and long-timers who had been at the same company for most of their natural lives, a level of interpersonal rapport emerged. The informal organization was reinforced in the lunchrooms and refreshed at the water cooler. We understood where to go for an analytic reality check or to get the real scoop on the corporate reorganization. On the personal side, we were regaled with stories of weekend regattas, koi fish collections, and the latest movie reviews. Beyond the work, there was the community of the workplace. Even those who eschewed the politics of corporate life were inevitably drawn into the circle of its personality.

The personality of your independent consulting practice is yours and only yours. You can broaden the interpersonal dimension of your business through aggressive networking and "face time" with the client, but being on the client site is different than being part of the client organization. You are not a part of it, you are apart from it, which brings me to the TAO of the consultant: Totally Alone Organizationally.

> Fundamentally, you are on your own. If you are going to climb the mountain, you best know who you are, what you are good at, and where you are going to need help. If there are two key attributes beyond those needed in your professional work, they are self-honesty and discipline. In most cases, you will not be able to delegate anything to anyone; it is all up to you. If you can talk yourself out of doing the ugly parts of your work, you are doomed. —*Dan Kleinman*

You must be able to look to yourself for direction, motivation, reinforcement, and consolation. Professional associations and colleagues can provide some of this validation, but for the most part, it is up to you. If you are not sure about your ability to work successfully in isolation, think back to your most hands-off manager. Did you feel neglected or comfortable in this role? How much structure do you need to prioritize and organize your work? Remember, as an independent, you will be able to take the time to make that happen.

> Timing is everything, and I'm talking here about the art of handling time. Try not to squeeze, stretch, or juggle your commitments when that energy can be better spent with regular, ongoing planning. Track your tasks for a couple of weeks to get an idea of how much time you spend on three or four or five of the most important things, then budget your time as you would budget your money. Leave yourself plenty of downtime and try not to sabotage yourself by procrastinating. At least once a week, sit down and spend a few minutes thinking about and/or writing down, then prioritizing your work tasks, adding an hour or so here and there to give yourself plenty of room for handling any crises that may come up. —*Hazel Payne*

Consider telecommuting experiences, where you may have spent time working from home: Were you as productive at home or were you more vulnerable to distractions? Moreover, were you rejuvenated when you reconnected with your colleagues personally? If the answer to these questions is an emphatic "yes," then the solitary path may not be the right one for you.

> It took time to build up a network of colleagues to spend time with; it can get lonely as an independent, and having people to exchange ideas and work on projects was a good way for me to structure my work and time. —*Carole Rehbock*

For this reason, many consultants go into business with another associate. Usually, they are consultants with complementary skills, rather than similar ones, in a field where two perspectives would be of value. For example, we have seen teams of strategic planners, where one partner had a service orientation and another a product focus; however, setting up a dual consultancy can have its own issues, such as conflicting interests or incompatible client management skills.

> The lessons learned in going out on my own were numerous and varied. I started my first consulting firm with a partner (I was a 51 percent owner) and utilized him for the technical piece. As it turned out, I was the reason clients signed on, I brought the exact business knowledge they needed, and his technical ability usually was an afterthought. This insight led me to sell him the business and go out on my own. —*Margery Mayer*

Issues around consulting partnerships could be the subjects of another book. Suffice it to say, for some, this approach can solve the isolation problem.

QUESTION THREE: THE "NO" FACTOR

In the management novella *The Five Temptations of a CEO*, Pat Leoncini posits that one of the most common fatal flaws of a CEO is the inability to deliver bad news. CEOs with this trait, and managers for that matter, don't want to tell people they are doing a bad job. To avoid that confrontation, they'd rather let them figure it out from the performance metrics than take the direct approach and, as the saying goes, "tell it like it is." Anyone setting up a consulting practice has become in effect the CEO of his or her own firm. Managing your practice with this flaw could be deadly.

Clients secure a consultant's services to assist with difficult decisions. By definition, judgment calls—and often downright ugly ones—will need to be made. Sometimes, the client is the last one to know how poorly a particular division, product, initiative, or manager is really performing. Implicit in the engagement of your service is a bond of trust, which says that you can be trusted to say what needs to be said. Many of the consultants that go into turnaround operations where most of the difficult questions can arise tend to understand this point. These individuals have been in failed enterprises and have experience with making tough decisions under fire.

Even in areas that are much less controversial, however, the "no" factor can manifest itself in insidious ways. Often, a client will engage a consultant to study problem X, but in the course of the inquiry, the client may ask for Y to be investigated as well. A good consultant must be able to say "no" to this addition. We are all trained in organizations to do whatever our boss tells us to do, but client management is different—to the extent that the engagement was to address problem X, doing more than that would be beyond the scope of the project. As such, it could affect your ability to complete the contractual obligation on time and on budget. The answer to the client needs to be "no." Any request to handle something beyond the original project should then be done as a separate project or an amendment to the original.

A related issue is coming to the recognition that the answer is not something that illustrates your expertise; rather it is the solution for the client. Many consultants we have talked to over the years admit that early on, they may have been too busy proving themselves to the client at the expense of improving the client's situation.

> When I first began consulting, I had an inordinate need to demonstrate my talents. Not only did it shut down listening; it also impacted my creativity. When you think you have all the answers, why do you need creativity? My first few engagements were spent doubling back over already traveled roads, listening a second time, collecting different data, and formulating new options. Since I charge by the project and not by the hour, I learned a financial as well as operational lesson. —*Dan Kleinman*

THE FINAL QUESTION: A PERSONAL ONE

Once you are comfortable with the first three questions, then it is time to get really practical. Can you afford to take this step now? What does your family think? Given the isolation factor, your family and friends may become far more central in your support structure professionally than they have been in the past. As such, consider carefully their thoughts. If your husband, wife, or partner is one of your biggest cheerleaders, then that can be a tremendous positive anchor.

Interestingly, the M^2 network includes a few husband-and-wife teams. These couples have made clear joint decisions about the priorities they want in their lives together. In one case, the couple assumes up to four months of downtime in their annual budgeting. As such, they don't burn at the rate they earn; rather, they stockpile for those leaner periods. Because their family economics are configured with these assumptions, their fixed family costs are maintained at a lower rate than others may assume. In lean times they are sure to get by, but in boom years they make a killing. Then again, what if your worst case happens and you get no business for one year, what would happen? Or more specifically, if something like that happened, why would it happen?

One of the M^2 specialist consultants is an expert in corporate risk management, in which he helps companies profile the risk of new ventures. He does this using a sophisticated, patented methodology of deliberately looking for disconfirming information. His premise is that most people naturally filter out the less-than-enthusiastic input and internalize the positive feedback when something new is being considered. Instead of discounting the negative, he suggests we explore it.

So, put yourself out one year. Your consulting practice has been a flamboyant flop; you have few clients and, by extension, meager income; and not only has your career path derailed, but there is also the opportunity cost of the road not taken. Now brainstorm all of the reasons why your consulting venture failed. Was it not enough marketing muscle, pricing, competition, or a total lack of interest in your expertise? Did you sacrifice standards and take projects that were below you and in that way adversely impact your reputation?

Be as creative as you can in trying to come up with a laundry list of reasons why you may have failed. Then rank the factors in terms of what is most likely to occur. Look then at that list: If it seems very likely that you would be compiling the same list next year, then stop now. If, on the other hand, it just doesn't ring true and you can't imagine these things happening, chances are that you have a great shot in the free-agent ranks.

> Starting and maintaining a business is not for the faint of heart. It requires a 150 percent commitment of time, energy, and money. It requires the ability to live with uncertainty. It requires a regular office, standard office hours, office equipment, and the willingness to do what it takes to get started and do good work. —*Sheila Wilkins, International Society of Performance Improvement Proceedings, 1999*

The idea of being on my own could be compared to jumping off a cliff for the first time, having no safety net. —*Margery Mayer*

Taking the consulting plunge is not unlike the first time you dive into a cold pond as a youngster. It's scary, and it can give a jolt for awhile. If you have marketable skills, tenacity, enjoy working with a variety of types of people, and can handle the inevitable financial and emotional volatility, it beats "working for a living." —*David Potter*

Chapter 6

MARKETING YOUR BRAND OF EXPERTISE

◆ PERSONAL BRAND MANAGEMENT 101

Now that you have decided the independent consulting career path is a logical one for you, it's time to create your brand. The marketers in the crowd may be nodding, and indeed may want to just skip to the next chapter, but some skeptics are probably thinking that building a brand is a lot of hype. For those who are tired of the constant onslaught of advertising from yet another Internet company and who equate brand building with that share of mind barrage, take heart. Building a brand for yourself is much more akin to creating your own business plan, which in the end will define your brand.

Your brand is, simply put, what you stand for and what you deliver to your clients. What are the tangible and intangible attributes that a buyer will assign to the services acquired from you? Studies of consumer product brands have established that the highest returns to investors were from those products with the strongest brand recognition and brand equity. By extension, the potential returns to your investors—primarily you—will be greatest the stronger your brand.

But branding is a different animal with consumer products; people don't have Energizer bunnies or theme songs or slogans. Or do they? "It's a good thing" has become the mantra of Martha Stewart, who is now one of the first personal, publicly traded brands. All of the Martha Stewart product sets are imbued with her characteristics of easy elegance, quality without exorbitance, and grace. You may not have a personal initial public offering (IPO) in your future, but you can aspire to be the Martha Stewart of your expertise category.

DEFINING CORE VALUES

> Marketing and selling consulting (intangible) services is the next major hurdle. It is essentially a process of product marketing, and most people do not know how to even approach this task. All of the aspects of marketing come into play. —*David Ellison*

The 1997 movie *Jerry Maguire* began with the main character establishing the core values for his independent business. He looked at the way the sports management game was currently practiced, and he developed a set of criteria for how, in his view, the work should be done. He didn't say how it would be implemented, and he didn't develop a tactical plan. Rather, he defined a set of governing constructs for the business in terms of how clients would be treated, competitors addressed, and objectives met.

To set up your own brand, you must define your own constructs or core values. What can I bring to this business, and what will make my brand better than the "product" anyone else can deliver? What will my work stand for at the end of the day? What will I unconditionally guarantee for my clients? What business will I not do, regardless of how slow the pipeline may be?

This last question can be a very telling one. In the early days of M^2, we worked on several significant interim management assignments with an independent treasury consultant. In one case, we matched her to an engagement with a large hospital system run by a not-for-profit corporation with ties to a religious order. Although she was passionate about the organization, its compassionate mission, and the challenge of the professional opportunity, she had to decline the assignment for personal reasons. An activist in the pro-choice campaign, she chose not to work for an organization that had even a remote connection to those on the other side of the choice debate. For her, the personal commitment to her convictions and the congruity of her personal and professional passions were key to her core values.

A CONSULTING SWOT

So, let's get down to work and begin the process. Defining your core values is like doing a mini-personal SWOT analysis, a strategy consulting acronym for strengths, weaknesses, opportunities, and threats.

In the strengths and weaknesses analysis, you are defining where you do and don't play in a functional discipline. For example, a former CEO may recognize that his or her true skills are in problem organizations, not maintenance or growth situations. You need to objectively critique your abilities in order to identify your true strengths. What are you exemplary at doing? Be brutally honest because your future business practice is riding on your self-analysis.

> Since going it alone, I realized how sought after my skills were and how much more successful I could be. The lesson I learned was to not underestimate my abilities and realize that my clients needed my independent and strategic view. My advice to others is to really access your strengths, document what you bring to the table, and try not to judge their value. Clients will quickly let you know which ones they value for their business needs. —*Margery Mayer*

Include not only your functional skills and experience but also your managerial and leadership skills to the extent that they are relevant to the type of projects and interim engagements you envision assuming. Client management, team-building, and other so-called softer skills have a marketability in the independent marketplace. Similarly, recognize experiential voids you lack in the weaknesses section. If you have never had profit-and-loss (P&L) accountability, international experience, or gone through an IPO and you are looking for interim CFO engagements, then any of these factors could impact your ability to sell yourself.

Your weaknesses are not only those things you don't do well because of experience or training but are also the things you don't like to do. It is a truism of human nature that you do best what you love.

> The biggest lesson for me was being clear about the work I wanted to do and not trying to do too many things. Although I saw myself as a management and organizational development specialist, I needed to get specific in talking with clients about the results I produced and the types of interventions that I had experience with. —*Carole Rehbock*

The opportunities section is where you can focus on your market in terms of future customers and prospects. Who will want to buy your intellectual capital? Where are the buyers located, and what would the buying process be?

The threats section is where you can think about why people wouldn't buy from you. Who are the non-customers in the market for my services? Because they need the product I am offering, if they won't buy from me, where or how are they addressing their need?

POSITIONING YOUR PRACTICE

Once you have completed this exercise, you are ready to truly create and position your brand. First, define the value proposition you will deliver to your target client. What is your niche?

> A niche orientation is a must for the successful independent consultant. A niche allows for the leveraging of time, expertise, and experiences. And for any independent consultant, it allows that consultant to work from his or her greatest strengths—said another way, from their comfort zone. —*Barry Deutsch*

From the value proposition, you can set a brand image appropriate for that target market. Your brand image is the look and feel of what you project on any marketing materials. It starts with your practice name and extends to business cards, brochures, tag lines, and proposals.

An event planner dealing in multimedia corporate meetings would develop a different brand image than one planning not-for-profit events. The former may want to project values of a corporate acumen, technological competence, and financial sophistication, whereas the latter may want to evoke social responsibility, creative execution, and cost consciousness.

This brand image should create an advantage for your practice in delivering your value proposition to your target client because it reinforces the message. For example, in the scenario described previously, a practice called The Corporate Meetings Group would already be positioned appropriately with the target CFO clients, who could be interested in having the annual shareholder meeting out-sourced.

In his book *Building Strong Brands*, David Aacker graphically illustrates brand positioning as the hub of the brand. The positioning supports the four spokes of the brand; it strengthens the value proposition, catches the attention of the target market, creates advantage in the sales process, and reinforces the brand image.

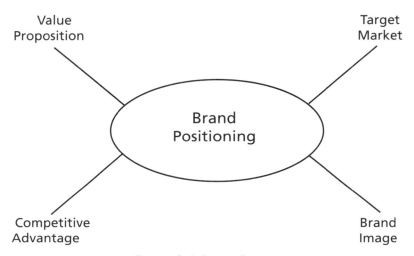

FIGURE 6–1 BRAND POSITIONS
(ADAPTED FROM D. AACKER, *BUILDING STRONG BRANDS*
New York: Free Press, 1996.)

M^2 consultants have done many creative things to leverage their brand. From simple things like e-mail and taglines to sophisticated capabilities pieces, the professionals know how to build a positioning that sells.

> One thing I find helpful is to ask previous clients to provide me with three to four sentences describing my value to them during an assignment. I then use those references as marketing information in newsletters, etc. For example, "I sleep better at night knowing Bill Meyer is managing the RFP process for the

purchase of our new ACD." Ms. Edie Heilman, President, Share Commercial Services, Inc., San Francisco. —*William Meyer*

An M^2 consultant developed a positioning exercise for clients to use in refining and tightening positioning statements. It is as simple as filling in the blanks in the following statement:

For _____(1) who _____(2), my brand/company is a _____(3) that _____(4). My brand is different from _____(5) because _____(6).

Where the blanks can be filled in with the following information:

1. Target audience
2. Client perception
3. Generic description
4. Key benefit
5. Competing products
6. Reasons why/attributes

To illustrate how this statement is used, here is how the M^2 team would fill in the blanks:

For decision makers with urgent business problems, M^2 is a source of independent talent that can solve those problems. M^2 is different from Internet sites because we offer the power of high technology leveraged by the insight of high touch delivered by senior professionals.

Critical in this example are the competing products. In fact, there could be multiple variations of the statement depending on the substitute product. Similarly, for an individual consultant, the positioning statement is very effective in clarifying the basis of competition. Take the following example of a public relations consultant.

> For service business CEOs who want more public and press visibility, PK Public Relations is an experienced PR expert who can get results in the press. PKPR is different from PR agencies because she handles the media personally, with agency-like sophistication, at the right price.

Of note in this example is that the competing good is a PR agency versus in-house PR operations. Were the key competitor the latter, the price would not be a key attribute in the buying choice.

The last positioning exercise is to be sure you have your "elevator pitch." This is the thirty-second "what do I do" soundbite that you may need to deliver to a client, a colleague, a cocktail party guest, or a perfect stranger in an elevator. An independent consultant never knows where the next project may come from. As such, you must always be ready with the concise statement of your positioning.

If you are in the technology world or the Internet space, be prepared to give an even more abbreviated version of this pitch. It's got to be compelling, comprehensible, and fast.

COMMUNICATING THE MESSAGE

Today, the résumé or curriculum vitae (CV) is the way you communicate your brand to its audience. Many consultants use brochures and marketing materials, but résumés are still the expected vehicle.

In putting together your brand résumé, be sure to consider a few things: Résumés aren't necessarily used to screen people into situations; they are used to screen people out. As such, a summarized version with the right information is far better than an exhaustive five-page document. With the former, a client may be intrigued and think potentially you have what he or she needs, whereas with the latter, if they don't see it somewhere (assuming they even read every page), then they'll assume you don't have the desired experience.

Also, you should reflect only the type of work, achievements, or accomplishments that you want to continue to pursue on an independent basis. If you have a financial background, which included auditing and then evolved into the mergers and acquisitions (M&A) world, where you discovered that deals are your passion, don't give much play to auditing on your résumé. Don't omit, but don't expatiate either. Early nongermane experiences can often be combined in clever ways.

Most important, remember in the New World of work that you are defined by your experience, not your job. Lead with your accomplishments, not with your employers. For verification purposes, be sure to include your employment history with the years of service. Your life is not IBM; your value is what you may have done for IBM while you worked there.

Many Internet consultant matching sites are developing unique skill representation tools meant to ultimately topple the résumé from its position of prominence in the world of work. This uprising may or may not be successful. If you choose to avail yourself of one of these services, then be sure to print a copy for yourself. See how your information is transformed into their template. You should always be sure you know how your expertise is represented to the world, or else you have lost control of your brand. Having established your core values, defined your value proposition, and positioned yourself in the marketplace, it's now time to join the new world of work.

Chapter 7

CHANNELING YOUR SALES

◆ IT'S TIME TO SELL

Armed with your new brand of expertise, it is time to begin selling your ideas and yourself. Ten years ago, the task ahead of you would be a long term, solutions sell. But now, the advent of the Internet age has changed all that. Nonetheless, it is important to pursue parallel sales paths to understand what types of engagement each avenue yields.

There are thee main sales channels to consider: direct sales, intermediaries, and independent contractor Websites. Only with the first channel are you in total control of your destiny; you choose the clients to go after, the type of project, its pricing, contractual covenants, and so on. Conversely, the first channel is also the most time intensive and creates the highest level of overhead because your unbillable time—your selling time—is in effect your overhead.

Intermediaries and Websites both can afford you with potential opportunities; however, you take more of a risk in terms of how well the projects fit your profile. With an intermediary, you may have more control over the nature of the project content, but the type of project and client is highly correlated to the marketing approach of the firm. Depending on the site, the Internet option is largely reactive, where the only control you have is whether to respond to a project.

Control is a factor that shouldn't be neglected because it often defines pricing and margin. Alternatively, what the intermediaries and Internet lack in control, they make up for in easiness. It isn't that difficult to create a digital or personal affiliation with an entity that, theoretically at least, can drive business your way.

If you consider the tradeoff of ease and control, the channels may map out such as in the following figure.

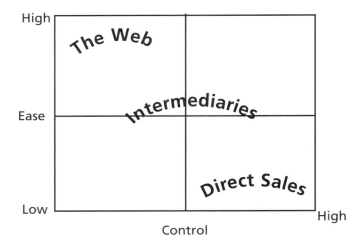

FIGURE 7–1 EASE-CONTROL DIAGRAM

So, let's discuss them one by one.

DIRECT SALES: THE POWER OF YOUR NETWORK

Direct sales is simply you going out and selling yourself. You meet potential clients at functions, prospect former colleagues, and constantly work a network of contacts until someone comes up with some work for you. For some people, this task is easier than it is for others.

Many of the most senior consultants in the M^2 network don't really "sell" at all. Their business comes to them through referral by virtue of their tenure in the business community. They affiliate with our firm, not so much to secure new projects as to secure different ones; what we may introduce to these professionals may be outside of their typical sphere of influence. Although they aren't selling directly, this mode isn't open to many people.

For most consultants, far more work is involved. Like any product or service, a consulting practice needs a sales plan, with target accounts and appropriate collateral. Many free agents have direct mail pieces that they send religiously to a targeted list of prospects. They work the industry trade groups and the Chamber of Commerce events continually to build their network of contacts.

> Most consultants are not very good at sales work. Getting a stream of jobs is a lot of work. The whole process is much harder and takes much more time and has much less success than it would seem at the beginning. My solution was to get help—lots of it. The first thing I did was to join a professional organization, the Institute of Management Consultants; it didn't provide very many leads on engagements, but it did provide lots of contacts that got me pointed in the right direction. The second thing I did was to join the M^2 network, through which I got several very good engagements. I will confess that I ultimately joined four other such networks, through which

> I got some leads but no real work. The third thing I did was to ally with a group of other, more established consultants; ultimately, I got quite a bit of work through them. But it was only after five years of consulting that I began to receive leads myself, from all the networking I had been doing. —*Jim White*

Without question, the toughest business to sell is your first project. Many new consultants market immediately to their prior employers, especially if the environment is one that often uses outside expertise. Others have tremendous luck and land something interesting right away.

Once some business is landed and successfully completed, there is new information to sell. Each engagement builds the consultant's repertoire of expertise. Each engagement also creates new opportunities to sell a similar engagement to a prospect.

> Philosophy: My next engagement is always predicated on the last engagement. My marketing extensions are my clients. In the last ten years, they have been generous enough to recommend me to others. And the pyramid continues to multiply. —*Dan Kleinman*

We represent many consultants who have built a practice on prior engagements. One of our investor relations consultants leveraged her prior treasury role into the investor relations field. As the IPO craze heated up, she made sure to handle an IPO from start to finish. Now she has turned this into her focus, taking a client through the IPO process and then moving on.

Sounds simple, right? For some people it is. This is where you must assess your personal selling aptitude and attitude. Many people love to sell and are good at it. Other competent experts hate to have to sell themselves. At M^2 we worked with a tremendously successful sales training curriculum developer (in essence, she wrote the book on how to sell) who really hated having to sell herself. It sounds counterintuitive, but it is true. For many people, selling is the downside of consulting.

> The biggest lesson I have learned as an independent consultant is that one can NEVER stop networking, even while occupied with live projects. Networking is essential to maintaining visibility in your marketplace and laying the groundwork for future projects. —*Janet Birgenheimer*

SALES 101

If you are new to the notion of sales, here are some quick tips to speed you on your way.

- *Time spent on reconnaissance is time well spent.* Make sure you know as much as possible about the companies to which you sell. Look up their Websites and review them thoroughly. Most clients nowadays expect a thorough review of their Website, and they would be insulted if you haven't gone over it carefully. For public companies, look up the analysts' reports on finance sites like dowjones.com or yahoo finance. For private companies, especially small ones, default to understanding their marketplace if primary information is scant. Look up public competitors to glean industry information. You should be well armed with knowledge of their products, markets, key competitors, recent acquisitions, market challenges, and so forth.

- *Remember you have two ears and one mouth, so allocate your time accordingly.* When in a sales interchange, rookies often think the most important dimension is to keep talking. It's not. The most important element on a sales call is to listen twice as much as you speak. This includes situations where you know the answers to some of their questions. We have had even experienced consultants give the client enough of an answer in the interview to enable the client to continue the work without outside expertise. One extreme situation was on a corporate identity project, where the task was to rename a long-time social service nonprofit, whose name had outlived its 1960s heritage.

The consultant, in attempting to demonstrate her creativity, came up with a name extemporaneously, which the concern opted to use. As a financially constrained grassroots organization, they apologized profusely but saw no need to deplete precious operating funds by continuing with the project. Listen, take notes, and listen some more.

- *Be nonaligned but politically astute.* All organizations, even tiny ones, have some undercurrent of politics. Try to discern what is going on in the organization to which you are pitching. Consider your own self-interest here. If it appears that a corporate overthrow is about to occur, then make sure you are talking to the winning side.

- *Sell your value and the benefits of your work.* This sounds basic, but many people lose their edge by selling features, not benefits. The fact that you have worked in e-commerce since the early days is a feature. The corollary that you know where the bodies are buried from the earliest Web initiatives is a benefit.

- *Understand it's not a job interview, it's a pitch.* Those who are new to consulting often fail to recognize that trying to secure a project is not the same as interviewing for a job. In a job interview, the selling is bidirectional. In a consulting meeting, the consultant is selling and the client is buying. In hot disciplines, the consultant may need to be sold on why it is an interesting project, but this is an exception, not a rule. Moreover, time has a different meaning, not to mention a cost implication. We once had a senior executive but rookie consultant lose a great marketing project because she told the client she could be up to speed on their business in three to four months. That's fine if you are a new employee on the job, but a client wants to buy immediate action if not immediate results.

- *Manage your farm.* The real estate world is perhaps the granddaddy of them all in terms of independent contractor sales. After all, every residential real estate agent is an independent contractor. We have all received the postcards and mailers from realtors announcing the sale, purchase, or listing of properties in the neighborhood. This is referred to as *farming.* Realtors farm an area until something grows. Some use many seeds, whereas others use just a few seeds and nurture them more carefully. The key thing, however, is to tend it. As you throw out your sales seeds, be sure to track, monitor, and regularly reconnect with all of those potential seedlings. At some point, any one of them may grow into a piece of business.

THE INTERMEDIARIES

Many firms consider themselves to be intermediaries in this new arena of executive- and managerial-level free-agent expertise. Some firms are appropriate for those only in a certain functional discipline or at a certain level of the organization. Many are purely regionally focused, whereas others are offshoots of large global temporary staffing concerns.

Kennedy Publications publishes an annual directory entitled *Temporary Placement Firms for Executives, Managers, and Professionals.* The directory lists hundreds of firms. Whether you call them an agency, a staffing company, a temporary executive firm, an interim management firm, or a consultant broker, they profess to do the same thing: represent you and your practice. But not all firms are the same.

A true intermediary in this new world of work understands its role as a partner to the consulting free agent. The firm is an additional marketing arm and, as such, has two clients to cultivate—the consulting population and the client universe. As a marketing arm, the firm must be able to sell the sophistication of each of the brands it represents, so a level of sophistication should be readily discernible in the process of an effective intermediary.

You need to decide what type of firm you want to represent your brand. Here are some differentiation points for you to consider in deciding which partners you may want to cultivate.

- *How core is management-level business to the firm?* The value of the intermediary to you is their ability to bring you interesting assignments. If a firm is primarily a traditional staffing firm, then most of the organizational resources, incentive structures, and attention will be focused on the core business, not the interim management or project side. By definition, these firms tend not to deal with complex business projects, so they are less facile in the intricacies of successful engagements of this sort. Therefore, the engagements these players may be able to introduce would be at lower levels of organizational responsibility and challenge.

- *Have they had projects in the past that would have been of interest to you?* The past is often a predictor of the future in terms of the type of engagements a firm may be able to secure. If you are looking for interim CFO work, then make sure the firm you ally with has a healthy history of interim CFO "gigs." Again, the selling sophistication of the right intermediary is critical.

- *Is the level of professionalism consistent with your expectations?* As you develop a relationship with a firm, evaluate every interaction in terms of the quality and level of service. To the extent that an intermediary is an extension of your business, is it one that you want representing you? Again, the truly professional intermediary understands the partnering relationship and extends that paradigm throughout its operations.

- *What is the "organizational heritage" of the firm?* This background can shape the service level of an intermediary firm. Most firms have a heritage in staffing, search, or consulting. Firms with roots in consulting or search often have a service-oriented approach. Conversely, those who come from staffing may not be as familiar with the decision-making processes of the types of buyers securing senior consultants and interim managers. M^2 has frequently had to work through master vendors at client sites where the master vendor was a staffing company acting as a contracting gatekeeper. The gatekeeper's limited access to the client, and this failure to appreciate the need for the consultant to interact directly with the buyer, was clearly detrimental to the process of finding the best talent for the role.

- *How does the firm define its services?* The jargon of a firm can set the tone for how it views the marketplace. As referenced previously, some of this focus comes from the heritage of the company and its founders. When M^2 describes our business, we talk about problems we have solved for clients, not contractors we have placed; our focus is on solutions rather than on staffing transactions. As such, a language distinction is interesting to note. The following table lists some of these terms:

Our Term	Other Terms
Engagement or "gig"	Job order
Consultant	Candidate or temp
Fees	Bill rate
Management conversion	Temp-to-perm

- *Does the firm specialize in marketing-related services at your level?* Most of these firms are focused on the creative side of advertising and promotion, offering freelance art directors, graphic artists, and copywriters. This is certainly a key industry need served by the likes of Acquent and Palladin, but more strategic, senior marketing consultants may find such firms too narrowly focused to yield interesting senior-level engagements.

- *What tasks will the intermediary perform for you?* Many different service levels exist in the various intermediary business models. Most firms make a match between consultant skills and client needs, but the handling of this task can vary. Some leave negotiations to the consultants, whereas others manage the pricing process. Some receive commissions from the consultant, whereas others are compensated by the clients. The best firms stay in touch with the consultant during the life of the engagement to assess its progress and to ensure that the project remains in scope and on budget.

- *What is the firm's billing process?* Some firms pay consultants on a W-2 basis, whereas others use a 1099. (See Chapter 8 for more on this topic.) Some firms handle all of the billing and collections, whereas others leave this sometimes daunting task to the consultants. Many free agents measure intermediaries not just by the caliber of the engagements but also by the strength of the financial organization, especially in terms of collections.

In short, you should learn many things about an intermediary before becoming part of its repository of talent.
Referrals from your colleagues are one of the most powerful
endorsements for a firm. Similarly, referrals from your clients
may also lead you to an exemplary interim management firm
in your space.

Figure 7–2 provides a map of the nationwide intermediaries
and where they play in terms of the level of the organization
and the scope of functionality.

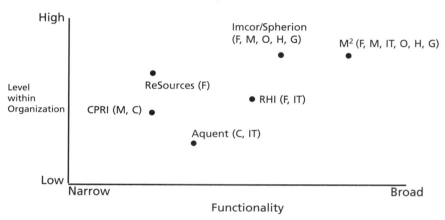

FIGURE 7–2 SELECTED TRADITIONAL INTERMEDIARIES

THE WEB WORLD

The Internet has spawned a whole new segment of intermediaries. Just as the heritage of a firm or its founder can
define the service level and sales niche of the firm, so, too,
does the heritage of the Web players. None of the current
free-agent Websites comes from the staffing world. Similarly,
few come from consulting. Most were born on the Web and
made for the Web, making them—by definition—technology
companies.

There are two main types of sites to consider: vendor matching sites and consultant matching sites. Vendor matching sites are those that provide business-to-business (B2B) services and include a professional services component; while you shop for telecommunications equipment or lease financing, you can also secure business consulting services. Sites of this type include envia.com, bizbuyer.com, and killerapp.com.

Consultant matching sites are designed for consultants; they offer content of interest to individual free agents regarding taxes, legal issues, and mobile computing. They have a project matching service that enables clients to post projects that can then be matched to your expertise. The larger sites include FreeAgent.com, Guru.com, and ICplanet.com.

A variation on the consultant matching sites are the auction sites. Here, consultants name a price and clients bid on it and vice versa. This business model is the least developed at this point, and the match activity appears to be low. The auction format mitigates some interesting aspects of the other sites, like the ability to figure out how much you may be worth. In a sense, the jury is still out on this mode of operation.

So, what are the advantages and disadvantages of the online marketing world?

Advantages

- It certainly is easy. Consultants can register with the various sites quite easily by entering a password and e-mailing a résumé. Some sites require only that a form be filled in.

- Projects can come from anywhere. Although this may be a liability for some consultants, it can represent an exciting opportunity for others.

- You can represent yourself in a new way. Some sites include personalized résumé creation or replacement tools, which potentially can represent an individual's skills in a far more powerful light.

- The site content can be helpful. To the extent that the consultant sites collect relevant information and present it in one place, there is a timesavings that shouldn't be under-estimated.

- Depending on how the site is laid out, you can get a sense of your market price. To the sense that similar consultants are listed and there are projects in your strike zone, you can see what type of pricing information is available.

Disadvantages

- The yield may be fairly low. Because both the vendor matching and the consultant matching sites are designed to encompass a quantity network versus a quality one, the actual number of projects that will come to you at this early stage in the technology can be low. (Technical consultants may have more robust experiences, however.)

- Personal networking is totally subsumed by computer networking. In other words, you can do little to affect the process, aside from having several versions of your résumé to exhaust every combination of buzzwords and keywords that may come up in fuzzy logic comparisons. The sheer size of the Internet intermediaries means that all transactions are by default algorithms, which depersonalizes the matching function; even though traditional intermediaries work with many consultants, there is still a sales manager, principal, or president with whom you can cultivate a personal relationship.

- You may need professional assistance to evaluate some of the services offered by the Internet matching agents. FreeAgent.com and Guru.com, for example, offer employment services, where they enable an independent consultant to be paid on a W-2 basis for tax purposes. There are many complex issues involved with this method, not the least of which is the loss of deductibility of certain business expenses. No successful consultant should surf into one of these programs without consulting his or her tax advisor on the specifics of the program first.

Table 7–1 outlines some of the large Internet sites, their current fees, and any special interest areas that may be relevant.

TABLE 7–1 INTERNET SITE DESCRIPTIONS

Company and/or Web Site	Service	Headquarters
Ants.com	Helps companies find freelance help as quickly as possible.	Santa Barbara, CA
Aquent Partners *www.aquent.com*	Combination traditional staffing business and online job-matching service.	Boston, MA
Elance.com	E-lancers bid auction-style for short-term company projects.	Sunnyvale, CA
eWork Exchange *www.ework.com*	Employers, staffing agencies, and project seekers decide what they want to pay eWork Exchange to obtain successful matches for short-term, off-site projects.	San Francisco, CA
FreeAgent.com	Matches independents with projects; sells insurance and administrative support packages.	New York, NY
FreeAgentNation.com	Provides advice and articles for e-lancers.	Washington, DC
FreetimeJobs.com	Helps small businesses find temporary help for short-term, part-time projects.	New York, NY
Guru.com	Matches independents with projects; offers extensive content and services.	San Francisco, CA
ICplanet.com	Hooks up professional and management-level contractors with hirers.	San Rafael, CA
iNiku.com	Matches IT and management professionals with projects; offers business support services through partners.	Redwood City, CA
SkillsVillage	Matches information-technol–ogy contractors with companies or staffing agencies.	Santa Clara, CA

Source: San Francisco Chronicle

It is too early to tell how this new avenue of networking may play out. As one consultant put it:

> I remember when I was in college in the 1970s, the pundits of technology evangelized two promises. The first was that by the time I was in my thirties, there would be a pill for everything—not to worry. The second was that while in my thirties, computers would be so prevalent and so functional that they would be doing almost everything for us. Each promise is well overdue in its fulfillment and realization. But we do see evidence in each of these areas of significant progress. The Internet is no different. It will be long on promises and very short on delivery. But not unlike the other two promises, billions will be spent on the development of the Internet. —*Dave Ellison*

In the interests of equal time, we asked one of these internet sites focused on independent consultants, Guru.com, to provide its view of this market. Please see the sidebar below.

GURU.COM

Certain people like to argue about whether or not technological advances make our lives better. You've probably heard them. Luddite pitched against technophile. Whether it's cellular phones, laptops, wireless devices, or the Net, some insist that technology makes our lives more complicated, while others firmly believe that technology simplifies. Such people have the luxury of this debate.

Independent professionals—contractors, freelancers, or "gurus" as we like to call them—must embrace technology to survive. Gurus have always embraced new technologies out of necessity. The laptop and cell phone are guru icons, and enable their independent lives. Technology democratizes how, when, and where gurus can work. Technology distributes work from inside corporate walls to the home offices of such gurus.

New technologies have played a significant part in giving rise to their breed. They are among the most tech-savvy people in the workforce, and the benefits of the Internet herald a renaissance for them. Gurus work independently because they seek to align the way they work and the way they live. Freedom and control are of primary importance. But they also desire "connection"— with peers, with information, with work. And the Net connects them.

One in six Americans now work outside of corporations. With 25 million Americans working independently today—more than double the number from 1990—there is a huge need for online resources. In the last year, a myriad of Websites catering to gurus have popped up. Some offer open marketplaces for connecting hirers with contractors, while others set up closed auctions for brokering services. There are Websites that overtly address the lifestyle of the independent professional, offering relevant products and services and advice on everything from how to work efficiently at home to how to deal with 1099 issues.

The rise of the Net has contributed to the rise of the independent workforce. The Net is bringing together thousands of professionals all over the world with companies that could not have found them otherwise. Furthermore, gurus are finding community and information online, and connecting to something larger than their solo practices. It's not just about getting projects, it's about e-mailing a kindred colleague halfway around the globe who may have shared the same problems.

And corporations are also getting into the act in droves. They're realizing that sometimes the best talent isn't found inside the company, but outside. They're using online resources by the tens of thousands, tapping into pools of contract talent rather than hiring full-time employees. As global boundaries evaporate in the Internet Economy and companies embrace the utility of the mobile workforce, the Net will be an increasingly efficient vehicle for finding talented people and getting work done. "Outsource" has become a business mantra.

The race of both companies and gurus online is also producing fierce competition for the attention of these customers. The best Websites will always keep the core interests of their customers at heart. Gurus want work, community, and information and services. Hiring companies simply want the best gurus, ASAP. Effectively balancing the needs of both parties will be challenging. The need of hiring companies to find the right guru fast and efficiently will drive opportunities for players in this market to innovate "hi-touch" extensions of their online products that help companies find the right guru faster. Ultimately, many of the businesses that best leverage the Net will be hybrid models that innovate the online/offline combination to make better matches. These companies will also have to remember that they're ultimately serving people, and that when people are looking to contract with people, it sometimes helps to have real people involved in making the match. (Imagine that!) After all, we're dealing with humans here, not widgets.

Independent professionals don't have the luxury of debating the usefulness of technology in their lives. It gave rise to their phenomenon. Ultimately, independent professionals and technological advancements are closely intertwined. They need each other and will feed off of each other. Both are instinctively adaptive. Both are required to innovate and are rewarded for it. Both have risked unpopularity to blaze new trails. The feast or famine nature of being independent is still a reality, but budding new technologies and new online services will provide a safety net to bring more consistency, efficiency, enjoyment, and reward to choosing the independent lifestyle. Someday in the not-too-distant future, we'll all be working a bit more like these trail-blazing gurus. We'll talk about "projects" instead of "jobs," we'll better align what we do with who we are, and we'll be happier doing it.

THE UGLY LITTLE EMPLOYMENT PROBLEM

WHO'S THE BOSS?

For those readers in the human resources field or the former CFOs in the crowd who may have dealt with the independent contractor versus employee problem already, feel free to skip this section. This chapter deals with a subject that is on the one hand incredibly dull, but on the other hand can be incredibly critical to certain clients at certain times.

The root question is: When you are working on an engagement with a client, for whom are you working? Put more precisely, who is your employer?

Most consultants would answer that they are in fact self-employed. The client is not the employer; the client is the customer. Unfortunately, although it seems obvious, it isn't that obvious in the eyes of the U.S. federal and state regulatory authorities.

Strange as it may seem, no employment law or regulation has ever defined what makes an employee, or more precisely, what makes someone a defensible independent consultant. In fact, this entire area of employment law is derived from English common law. The main tenets come from master-servant relationships as defined in the thirteenth century, when the bubonic plague decimated most of the population and required clarification of who is a master and who is not. So, although we all know the world of work has changed dramatically since the days of vassals and serfs, employment law has not.

The problem arises for many independent consultants because of ambiguity. Without an incontrovertible definition, anyone providing services to a company could be deemed an employee. At the heart of the issue is economic value; wherever there is an employment relationship, there must be employment taxes. As such, state and federal authorities are often overzealous in tracking down any situations that could potentially yield tax dollars. The IRS states that in collecting taxes, it receives 99 percent of the taxes due from payments collected via employers through withholding taxes. In the case of those among the ranks of the self-employed who file income taxes quarterly, only 75 percent of the taxes are remitted. Let's be serious now—it's not about employment, it's about tax revenue.

Let me offer an outlandish example, which I experienced personally when testifying on this issue in front of the California State Senate in 1996. The California Employment Development Department (EDD) is known nationwide for being one of the most difficult (some may say Neanderthal) employment regulators in the nation. An insurance broker testified to a California Senate committee that he had been unduly fined by the EDD for employment taxes due. Apparently, the broker had made many large payments to a payee listed as "Hartford." This payee was, of course, the Hartford Insurance Company, one of the major lines carried by the broker. An EDD auditor assumed that Hartford was an outside contractor (the auditor was obviously not insured by Hartford) and penalized the insurance broker. Finding that the broker had an "employment" relationship with Hartford, the EDD assessed the man hefty fines calculated on all of the premium dollars that had been paid to Hartford. "Over-zealous" may be an understatement in this case.

In fact, the small business lobby has cited this issue as one of the top business regulation problems in all of its most recent summits. The fines and penalties heaped on the companies who may be using an outsider inappropriately are onerous. They are hefty because implicit in their calculation is the notion that not only were payroll taxes unpaid, but income taxes were probably unpaid as well. The penalty is calculated with both of these tax rates, often using the maximum income tax rate as the penalty threshold. Fines can be reduced if an employer can show that the contractor indeed paid his income taxes, but companies do not usually require this information from consultants who work with them.

As for you, the consultant who is found to have been an employee, the penalty is not onerous so much as it is annoying. Certain deductions you may have taken against income as an independent contractor may be disallowed, causing you to have to refigure your income, refile your taxes, and pay interest on any underpayment of tax. Depending on the size of your disallowed deductions, this could be a big number. KEOUGH plans may be disallowed as well, which could result in an additional $30,000 of taxable income. Furthermore, if your client is penalized, you may face a damaged relationship with a source of your business.

The ambiguity in employment law means that your status as an independent professional could be called into question at any point in time. Incorporating yourself can ease the burden of proof, but it does not eliminate it. You should consult your lawyer to understand the implications fully. But be advised that the existence of a contract stating the fact that you are not an employee of your client is not enough. The nature of the work and the way in which it is structured and coordinated by the client can create a semblance of employment that could obviate the most adroitly crafted contract language.

SO WHY DO I CARE?

Many large companies, especially those in the technology sector, are so gun-shy about this issue that they no longer allow individuals to receive payments, requiring all to go through a third-party vendor. Temporary staffing companies have built master vendor empires, where they handle the "payrolling" of independent consultants, making the consultant a temporary employee to enable a clear employment status. Where once this was an issue only for technical consultants and independent programmers, it has now become a much more mainstream problem.

In 1997, this somewhat abstruse employment issue hit the front page as Microsoft was found liable for the misclassification of workers. To paraphrase an old saying, "as General Motors goes, so goes the nation." The idea that the maxim is better stated with Microsoft as the all-powerful corporation, rather than General Motors, is a telling statement about the composition of the U.S. economy. With all due respect to GM, the knowledge sector has supplanted manufacturing.

To many people in the knowledge sector, the decision by the U.S. Court of Appeals against Microsoft was chilling. The federal court ruled that hundreds of workers Microsoft had classified as independent contractors were in fact common-law employees and therefore eligible for participation in the company's 401K and stock purchase programs. This ruling stood on appeal, which sent another shudder through the white collar world. Given the widespread usage of independent contractors in the knowledge economy, reports suggested that the negative ramifications could be significant . . . or could they?

The implication has been made that by virtue of these decisions, any independent contractor may be entitled to benefits; however, that interpretation is far too simplistic. From the description, it appears that Microsoft did indeed misclassify workers; they violated the truest of all tests of employee status—right to control. Contract employees designated as independent contractors were closely supervised by Microsoft employees and performed the same work as other employees in the same offices with the same badges. Moreover, they held routine jobs such as software tester and proofreader.

Microsoft made a mistake, and like GM, it tried to reverse itself, but the recall did not work. Once they were found at fault by the IRS in 1990, Microsoft changed its mode of operation and began running independent contractors through temporary agencies. One particular group of independent contractors refused to become temporary employees and created the class-action lawsuit that led to the recent decisions.

The Microsoft case begs the larger question of how there can be such a discrepancy between the governmental interpretation of the regulations and the company's posture. If Microsoft and its legions of attorneys couldn't effectively address this classification risk, how can individuals and companies attempt to comply?

To understand your risk in this area better, you need to understand some of the ways in which the government looks at the issue. Although there is no clear law, there are some vague guidelines published by the IRS, frequently referred to as the "20 Points." These 20 points have recently been distilled into the following three main areas of concern:

1. *Behavioral control.* Who has the right to control the worker? If a company retains the right to dictate the work conditions, hours, locations, and/or methodology, or if training is required, then the worker should be an employee.

2. *Financial control.* Does the worker have a financial stake other than hourly wages? Hourly wages are an indication that the relationship should be an employment situation;

however, if a project fee with incentives for early completion is provided, then this arrangement indicates an independent businessperson.

3. *Relationship of the parties.* What is the contract like? Are there implied benefits that are generally offered only to employees? Does the consultant have multiple clients, and is he or she able to continue those relationships? Is there an assurance of continued employment? If the client company is the consultant's only source of income, and the consultant has no contract and occupies a company parking space, chances are that the consultant would be considered an employee.

The nature of the work pursued by many senior management consultants is often above reproach based on these three issues. Many marketing research consultants, for example, especially in this day and age, work remotely from their own offices. Similarly, many consultants assume assignments with more than one client concurrently.

Unfortunately, except in strategy and business planning engagements, most consulting projects are billed at an hourly or daily rate rather than for a contract fee. This stems from the fact that business executives are used to paying their professional services providers (i.e., lawyers and accountants) by the hour. When companies began securing services in other disciplines, the hourly pricing structure seemed comfortable and understandable; however, hourly fees are not necessarily a red flag in and of themselves. Looking at all three concern areas, here are some situations that may create a suggestion of employment to the IRS or its state cognates.

- Long-term, dedicated projects that may be regularly extended could signal a promise of employment.

- Interim engagements where the consultant is filling the role of an employee and being directly managed (and controlled) by the client staff, or alternatively acting as the manager of the client staff.

- Similarly, interim engagements or projects where the consultant is handling the same work or doing the same job as a regular management employee.

Moreover, although it isn't cited in the IRS distillation, another area of concern is when interim managers have either profit-and-loss responsibility, hiring and firing authority, and/or any fiduciary obligations to the enterprise.

If these aren't the types of engagements that you envision taking, then here are some ways to further bolster your practice from annoying problems that may arise from this issue:

- *First and foremost when starting your practice, be sure to get sound legal and tax advice about the various forms of practice governance.* Although creating and running a corporation for an individual can create tremendous overhead, it can also mitigate significantly the vulnerability to some of these issues. The separate business tax identification, which is a by-product of a corporate governance structure, is a routine indicator for some clients that classification is not a problem.

- *Always have more than one client.* Similarly, take pains to demonstrate that you are offering your services to the community at large. A unique business name, a separate office, equipment, advertising and collateral materials, or assets that are owned by the business are critical factors. All of these things contribute to the image that you are running a business, not merely being employed tacitly by another company.

- *Finally, take control over your work circumstances.* Don't let a client set your hours for you. Keep in mind that you have been hired to achieve a result; how you do that needs to be up to you.

If you are in the situation where the type of work you assume would most likely be in the gray area and/or a clear case of looking like an employee, here are your options.

- Verify with tax and legal counsel whether you can address the situation through incorporation.

- Consider becoming a part of the client's payroll.
- Find an employer for yourself.

SO I NEED AN EMPLOYER

Now, thanks to the Internet, there are a host of options for free agents and consultants who may need to be employed. There are firms like Consultant Billing Inc. (CBI), a firm started by the M^2 team solely for the purpose of being able to employ consultants when they needed an employer. In the case of CBI, the client firms, recognizing that they are diminishing their risk of reclassification by the IRS, pay a bit more for an individual's expertise. The additional margin covers the statutory payroll taxes required. The independent consultant becomes a CBI employee for the duration of the assignment and receives a W-2 at year-end. Unlike 1099 consulting fees that are paid in full, income taxes are withheld and FICA taxes are assessed.

In some cases, having an employer can be beneficial for a consultant. As a self-employed individual, you must pay the entire portion of the FICA burden, or 15.3 percent of your self-employment income. As an employee, your employer pays half or 7.65 percent. Additionally, you would be covered by workers' compensation insurance as well as unemployment insurance. Finally, many of the employer service providers will enable you to secure some level of benefits, whether it be health insurance, 401K access, or other features; however, not all employers are the same. Keep the following key issues in mind.

- *When you give up your independence and become an employee, even if only for the duration of an engagement, you are still due certain rights.* The most salient is the right to be paid no later than 10 days following the completion of a pay period (no longer than one month) of work. Some of the Internet service providers suggest that you will be paid as their employee when your client pays them. If that window does not coincide with the legal requirement, then that potential employer may be breaking the law. As such, ensure that the payrolling arrangement you secure is legal.

- *Understand the costs your employer is passing on to you.* At the very least, you will experience a significant reduction in net pay, or cashflow, due to withholding taxes. Be sure to get a detailed breakdown of what services they will be providing you for what type of fee.

- *Also, understand that you can't have it both ways.* We have seen independent contractors who enjoy the cashflow benefits of the independent mode and are fully cognizant of the benefits tradeoff, who then file for unemployment. If you are an independent contractor, you are not entitled to unemployment by definition, so filing for unemployment is wrong. These frivolous claims don't appear to get the same attention. Often these filings trigger audits of the alleged employer, so be aware that you could also create problems for your clients. The IRS and states regulators are more intent on landing the "big fish," so they don't seem to appropriately penalize the independent contractors who try to have it both ways. They should.

- *Finally, be attuned to political developments on this front.* This whole chapter would have been unnecessary if U.S. legislators could act together to establish appropriate regulations in this area. Now that you know, keep abreast of ongoing lobbying and new legislation. It's time that employment law caught up with the Internet age.

chapter

9

AND NOW TO THE NITTY GRITTY

GET IT IN WRITING

So, you've made your decision about how you will reflect your consulting income on your taxes—the 1099/W-2 choice. Now, you are ready to start an engagement. What else might you need to know? Or, more specifically, what other differences might you expect from life as an employee?

Well, working for a client is not the same as working for an employer. For one thing, the basis of the relationship is completely different. As discussed in the last chapter, the basis of employment law stems from master-servant relationships where the company is the master and the employee is the servant.

Consulting projects or interim assignments are conducted on a fundamentally different premise. It is a peer-to-peer relationship, where explicitly each party has something to gain from the term of the interaction. The client gains the result desired, and the consultant earns fees. (Theoretically, this same mutual aggrandizement exists in employment relationships, but at best it is implicit.)

By extension, if the desired result is not achieved, then the other party need not pay the fees due. To protect yourself, you need an effective contractual agreement. Again, for your own specialty, be sure to consult legal counsel; an independent bridge designer will have far more complexity to his contract than will an interim marketing manager.

Contracts need not be long and arduous, and depending on your particular area of expertise, yours could be quite simple. Most independent consultants simply use a letter format that includes certain key terms and provisions. The key difference from a standard letter, however, is that it should be countersigned by the client. Having it in writing is good, but having them sign off on it is better.

The important points to make in a contract, memo of understanding, or agreement letter are highlighted in the following sections.

A PROJECT DESCRIPTION

Being as precise as possible, you need to outline what the assignment entails. Include the scope of the project; that is, areas to be covered as well as areas that will not be addressed. In the case of interim engagements, be sure to itemize any areas in the job description that will *not* be handled as part of the project. In some interim situations, for example, hiring decisions may be deferred until the regular employee manager is on board.

To the extent that the accomplishment of the project requires the client to dedicate some resources to your effort and/or to provide access to information or key employees, you should cite this need. To the extent that the client's failure to perform any of these tasks would impair your work product or your ability to complete the work in a timely manner, that condition should also be stated.

Finally, be sure to include the form for the final deliverable. Will it be a written report or a presentation? Whereas you may think a 15-slide PowerPoint presentation captures the essence of your work, your client may require a 45-page report.

FEES AND PAYMENT TERMS

Outline the fees that have been negotiated for the project, including the expected timing of payments. If you intend to calculate late charges on delinquent fees, include that condition as well. For pricing calculated on a percent-of-completion basis, be sure to outline clearly how the percentages will be determined and validated.

In the case of hourly or per diem billing rates, one area that may warrant explicit mention is the compensation for travel time. If you will be traveling at length, specifically via air, be sure to negotiate a reimbursement rate for your time. A good rule of thumb is your ability to work en route. If you can work while traveling, then you should be able to bill the time. If not, then you should be able to bill some percentage (25 to 50 percent) because the time on the plane was time for which you were unavailable to other clients.

In the event that expenses will be reimbursed, at the very least include the fact of reimbursement. The best treatment is to provide an estimate of expenses, along with a breakdown of typical hourly expense costs.

Similarly, for engagements that require significant travel and temporary living situations, be specific regarding the details of these arrangements. Will the client pay for the housing directly or will you be accorded a housing allowance? If by doing a five-month gig overseas, you will want to return home twice during the engagement and your client has agreed to that stipulation, be sure this condition is clear in the engagement letter or contract.

For international engagements, be sure to specify the currency and country in which you expect to be paid. For some of our international engagements, we coordinated wire transfer disbursements in U.S. dollars for expatriate consultants.

RELATIONSHIP OF THE PARTIES

If you are conducting the project on an independent contracting basis, then say so in your agreement. State that you are not an employee and expect no workers' compensation, unemployment insurance, or any other benefits that may be provided to employees.

Similarly, if you are conducting the project through a payrolling service (see Chapter 8), then outline that as well. Explain that as an employee of XYZ Payrolling, you understand that you are not an employee of your client and are therefore not entitled to receive the benefits typically accorded to employees.

Finally, make it clear that there are conditions under which the project and or relationship can be terminated. Keep in mind that under contract law, if you don't deliver a result, then you need not be paid. Think of the agreement in terms of tradespeople, because those are the disciplines that the law was originally designed to govern. If you hire a contractor to paint your house and he does not complete the job, chances are that you could withhold payment. After all, what good is a house with only three sides painted? The analogy applies to your work as well. If you don't deliver what you say you will, then you may not be entitled to payment either. As such, you may want to consider a termination or cancellation clause, which gives the client notice and informs the client of what level of payment would still be due under the agreement.

INTELLECTUAL PROPERTY

More and more, intellectual property has become a key issue in consulting contracts. As an independent consultant, your work product is your own, unless it is stipulated otherwise. As an employee, your work product is your employer's, on the basis of the "work for hire" body of law. Many clients require an independent consultant to cede ownership rights to them. This can be done simply by describing the project as a work for hire. Alternatively, you can specifically state that you assign all ownership rights to your client. You can also offer clients a license, either perpetual or discrete, so that the client can share in the ownership.

Many consultants do not want to give up their intellectual property even if it means losing a client. For those who want to be sure that their ownership is clear, even though common law says that as an independent you own it, you should specifically assert your ownership in the agreement.

Conversely, many clients are even stricter in their interpretation of intellectual property law. Some companies, especially in the entertainment industry, insert *droit morale* clauses, where a consultant is asked to cede not only ownership rights but moral rights to an idea as well. If, for example, a consultant worked at Disney and thought it would be great to see Mickey Mouse with a moustache and that version of Mickey Mouse becomes a licensing bonanza, then by having ceded his or her moral rights to the moustache idea (something Disney would no doubt require), the consultant would not be entitled to reap any of the gains from the increased revenue derived from that whimsical change.

This is an issue primarily for those in the creative domain, a realm that is growing. If you are on the idea side of a business problem, then be sure to consult your attorney if your client wants you to waive your moral rights.

A corollary to intellectual property is nondisclosure agreements, which are often referred to as NDAs. Many technology companies today require NDAs from any management-level outsider involved at a strategic level. A typical NDA requires the signer not to divulge trade secrets, patents, or proprietary information to anyone outside the company. Many people disregard NDAs because many of the provisions often end up unenforceable in court. This may be true, especially in California, but nonetheless, a well-crafted NDA can be a powerful protection. If your client can prove that you intentionally violated the agreement, then they may be entitled to injunctive relief, damages, and even compensation for lost profits.

Your exposure in signing an NDA, assuming that you don't intend to divulge trade secrets, is related to the specificity of the information that is being protected and whether you may accidentally impinge on the NDA covenants. If the language is vague and/or your knowledge of the information could have been acquired in other private or public ways, then think twice before you sign the agreement. At the very least, work with the client to rein in the scope of the NDA coverage to make it more protective for them and less likely for you to violate inadvertently.

OTHER CONTRACTUAL THOUGHTS

Many consultants include indemnification provisions to protect against the horror of an absolute failure. The best indemnifications are those that are mutual. Your client holds you harmless from liability in certain cases, and you do the same for them. Such protective clauses are best drafted with legal assistance or at least reviewed by a lawyer who specializes in the area.

Another potential inclusion would address possible litigation, or more specifically the avoidance of such an occurrence. Mediation and arbitration sections or both are becoming far more common in consulting agreements. In either case, you may want to be sure—and this is especially true if you are signing a client's contract—that there is limited discovery. Discovery, of course, is the time-consuming and expensive part of the litigation process, which involves collecting information in many ways, including orally, which means depositions. Depositions are expensive because the attorneys from both sides must attend all depositions. Asking for arbitration in lieu of litigation does no good if they have unlimited discovery and can depose every client or coworker you have ever had. Again, when in doubt in this area, consult a lawyer first, so that you can avoid consulting them later.

Keep in mind also that contracts are living documents. In negotiating agreements with clients, you will often identify loopholes that expose you to liability or clauses that are too one-sided and unfair by definition. Make it a practice to revise your agreement template regularly to reflect the newfound knowledge you gain with each negotiation. Similarly, think about your contract in isolation from the rest of your business. Securing errors and omissions coverage for your business, for example, may obviate the need for strong indemnification language.

Finally, all of this presumes that your client will be comfortable using your agreement. More often than not, you may be asked to execute the clients' standard third-party agreement. Don't try to negotiate in all of your points; just be sure to understand the implications of all of theirs. Many third-party contracts require you to carry levels of insurance coverage that are not applicable for an individual. I have personally explained to many clients why an independent consultant cannot be covered by workers' compensation. This class of coverage is offered to companies only, so an individual, by definition, is not eligible. Companies are often willing to negotiate on those points.

NAME YOUR PRICE

◆ IT'S A MARKET OUT THERE!

Pricing is an esoteric science. In fact, the M^2 network contains several Ph.D. statisticians and/or economists with expertise in price theory. Pricing your services need not require a doctorate in applied mathematics, but it does require some thoughtful considerations. Perhaps the most important consideration is that the driving constraint does not involve you or what you think you should make; rather, the most important consideration is what the market rate is for your services.

Many senior management consultants scoff at the notion of a market price because such economic models are typically applied to commodity businesses. Interim CEOs are not pork-bellies and aren't fungible, so by definition they are unique goods and bear a unique price structure. Although I agree with the porkbelly analogy, the truth of the matter is that market prices are set for bundles of goods, including their substitute products. If one relaxes certain assumptions, a whole host of individual practitioners could be seen as sub-stitutes for one another, and hence a market price can form.

In fact, in 1994, we not only discerned a market, but we also saw it move. In 1994, California was still in the trough of a recession. Doubly stung by corporate downsizing and the wholesale closure of more than one dozen military bases across the state, unemployment was high, spirits were down, and the job outlook for many people was grim. In January, we found a senior technical recruiter for a semiconductor man-ufacturer. Shortly thereafter, other clients asked for a similar level of senior, technical search expertise. In the course of six months, we received so many requests that the ranks of the senior technical recruiters were entirely depleted.

We saw the price rise from $60 per hour to nearly double that in the course of six months. When the talent was at its most scarce point, our original semiconductor client called us back and asked us for an additional resource. We explained that the price would now be $120 per hour, and he was hor-rified; he said that he wanted a consultant at the same price as his first consultant. It wasn't until we said we'd have to walk away from the project because we just couldn't help him at that kind of fee structure that he understood the reality of the situation. He felt better when we suggested that he was a successful arbitrageur because his initial $60-per-hour resource would command much more in the current marketplace.

In 20/20 hindsight, this market move was the first sign that the California economy was about to recover from its extended economic malaise. It was also the evidence of the existence of a senior-level talent market. Even though recruiters differ (i.e., the folks who find software developers don't deal with board-level designers or testing engineers), the entire market segment was in such demand that the price shifted across the board.

As in any market, there is never just one price. The best coffee beans sell at a premium to those that are less ripe or inferior in some other way. (I suppose there is a similar analogy with porkbellies, but I just don't want to go there.) Similarly, there can be distortions caused by peaks in demand or shortages in supply that stem from exogenous sources. A drought in Sumatra may reduce the supply of those beans and thereby increase the price of Kenyan coffee.

Because the expertise market is far less homogenized than coffee beans, a better analogy is housing. Anyone who has ever bought or sold a house understands the idea of market comparables. Except in nondescript subdivisions, no two houses are alike. The seller, typically via a broker, must sort through the recent sales data to identify those properties most similar to the one to be sold. Adjustments are made to comparables to allow for differences in square footage, yard size, garages, or amenities. This analysis yields what the apparent market value of a home may be.

Interestingly, the actual sales price may differ dramatically. It could be that the particular neighborhood falls out of favor, so home values there drop 10 percent. Alternatively, there might be a buyer who really wants to live on a particular street and will pay anything for a house with the requisite address.

The expertise market is similar because no two people have exactly the same background. Degrees from different schools of similar caliber can vary dramatically; just look at the University of Chicago MBA program versus the Stanford MBA program. The former is replete with the differential equations underpinning the Black Scholes option pricing model, whereas the latter grooms the Silicon Valley entrepreneurial elite.

Just like the person who always wanted to own a home on a certain street, some clients will pay more for a pedigree from a different institution. Similarly, certain employment backgrounds have cache, like Procter & Gamble for marketers or Yahoo in the e-commerce realm.

Inside information can distort market prices as well. People on the inside of Oracle understand the stringency of the screening process that precedes anyone being hired as an employee. Running this gauntlet successfully can have a value to Oracle alumnae.

IT'S THE WORK, STUPID!

When Bill Clinton ran for president in 1992, one of his campaign mantras was "It's the economy, stupid." In other words, any other national issue paled in comparison to the primacy of economic health.

For independent consultants, there is a similar mantra: "It's the work, stupid." Many consultants, veterans and rookies alike, sometimes lose sight of the fact that fees aren't determined by an individual's value, credentials, or financial straits. The price of work should depend on the value delivered to the client.

We have had individuals billing dramatically different fees concurrently to different clients. One was a CFO who did some economic modeling for a bank at one rate and was a part-time interim CFO at another. The latter engagement warranted higher fees because of the fiduciary obligations and management responsibilities of the position. Although some people may see this rate fluctuation as opportunistic, it's more a sign of efficient markets.

The difficulty here, though, is discerning the market price. In some cases, clients have a good idea of the price. Intermediaries like M^2 are typically knowledgeable about the relative value of skill sets and what minimum skill sets would be required to achieve a desired result.

Given the ambiguity, here are some rules of thumb:

- *Risk is proportionate to return.* The more risky a project, whether the risk stems from an aggressive goal or a tenuous business proposition, the more it should pay. Turnaround situations are a perfect example. The potential for failure is high, so the reward for success should be proportionately high as well.

  Similarly, a project where the consultant assumes an economic risk by virtue of a fixed fee may warrant a higher equivalent per-hour fee. Such proposal-based, fixed-fee projects often involve a substantial investment in time to develop the context for the proposal, in addition to the standard marketing cost for finding the engagement.

- *Capital formation is worth an investment.* This maxim cuts both ways. If a client is buying you for your unique knowledge of a particular field or process and the client is expecting to own those intellectual capital rights, you may be owed a premium. You are leaving behind with your client a valuable asset—the output of your brainpower. Alternatively, any engagement that enhances your intellectual capital is worth doing potentially at a discount. Because new skills can beget new engagements, a project that promises to significantly build your own self-worth should be priced accordingly.

  The advent of e-commerce was such a watershed development that it forced many senior consultants to reevaluate their own fee structures. In the early days, not many people had Internet experience. More and more clients were asking for such a background, and the senior consultants knew it. Any opportunity to build that aspect of an individual's repertoire was seen as an opportunity to play in an increasingly exciting and lucrative marketplace. We saw interim CFO consultants discount fees by more than 40 percent just to get the opportunity to add a key skill to their already accomplished backgrounds.

- *Cabs and cars charge differently.* In his book *Interim Management*, Dennis Russell makes a great analogy about pricing the interim business in the UK. He likens the pricing decision to the difference in per-mile fees of a cab versus a car.

> Compared to the rigidities of an open-ended employment contract, clients should—and will—pay a premium for you being available (flexibly) and able to carry out their assignment now. Think of the cost per mile of running a car you own—say £.25—and compare that with taking a taxi—say £2.50. A 10 times factor! Yet, perfectly sensible people rent cars and take taxis. Why? Because they know there is a competitive market for these services that keeps a measure of control on the price—and because, on balance, the premium for convenience outweighs the cost. —*Dennis Russell,* in *Interim Management*, p. 55.

Because a cab is a short-haul, highly convenient, and totally dedicated resource, it is more expensive per mile. Similarly, if you are pricing a 20-hour project versus a 20-month project, the price per hour needs to be substantially different in both cases. In the former, you need to build in a risk premium to reflect the fact that you will be looking for yet another project in one month's time. In the latter instance, there can be a discount because there is so much guaranteed income. So, when pricing any assignment, develop long-term as well as short-term fees.

- *Convenience has a price for the consultant, too.* Similarly, there is something to be said for a client that is across the street. The life of a consultant incurs undeniable wear and tear. Any attribute of an engagement that mitigates this hardship should be weighed in the pricing calculus.

- *The one percent rule helps.* Dennis Russell also developed the one percent rule as a pricing algorithm for interim managers in the UK. He shared it with me two years ago, and ever since we have been tracking it loosely. It appears to hold in the United States as well. This rule says that a person's daily fee should be one percent of what that individual should make in salary in one year. The salary level should be placed at the market price for that type of employed role, rather than a specific offer. For example, a marketer who wants to make $100,000 per year should charge $1,000 per day, or $125 per hour. A more junior human resources manager hoping to make $60,000 per year could command $600 per day and $75 per hour as an HR generalist consultant.

SETTING YOUR PRICE

In general, pricing is calculated in one of four ways: an hourly fee, a project fee, a success fee, or an equity deal. The first is by far the most prevalent pricing structure. Clients are used to paying professional services providers, such as accountants and lawyers, by the hour, so they pay consultants by the hour, too.

Per diems are often used in situations where a client is concerned about overtime and doesn't want to pay for work being done ten hours per day. The natural extrapolation here is the monthly billing, where again, the individual extra hours are not reflected. In truth, this pricing nuance is not material. For the type of engagements that could be paid monthly, an hour here or there to the consultant will not matter. These tend to be long-term, highly compensated senior-level engagements.

A variation on monthly fees is a retainer-based payment. This is typically used in situations where the time requirement in an interval is uncertain. The client may need you 40 hours in one week and zero the next. The best way to price such a retainer structure is to set a specified "not to exceed" level for the hours in any given retainer period. Otherwise, this type of arrangement could be highly uneconomic for a consultant.

Project fees are usually used in the strategy world, whether it is general business, technology, or marketing strategy. Consultants who bill in this way are typically proficient in estimating the time it will take to achieve a result. They are also clear about the deliverables from the outset. Project fee arrangements suffer when a dispute occurs between the client and the consultant as to what the final deliverable is to be.

Success fees are typically used only in the financial arena for projects that are involved with raising capital. In these cases, clients typically pay some amount of the money raised. More sophisticated consultants use a reverse Lehman formula, whereby the percentage they receive is higher, the more money is raised.

Finally, especially in the frenzied world of today's Internet economy, equity-based fees are currently popular. In this case, a consultant takes some form of equity, whether stocks, options, or warrants, as a portion of fees. We recommend to our consultants who are interested in this pricing structure to—first and foremost—consult their tax advisors, but then we suggest that the compensation include at least enough cash to cover the tax liability. Remember, even if a stock is pre-IPO and highly undervalued, it has some valuation upon receipt. That value will be your basis in the stock and will be reportable as income in the year received.

Another word of advice on stock deals is that, in any type of stock portfolio, diversification is key. Don't collect all your fees in stock; charge some in cash. Of those fees that you take in stock, make sure you are diversified in different economic sectors.

In our case, M^2 will take equity in lieu of our fees; however, we use the venture capital investors as a proxy for credit quality. A marquee venture capitalist is like a Good Housekeeping seal of approval; we'd much rather take equity in a deal that has been funded by Kleiner Perkins or Hummer Winblad than in a company funded by anonymous investors.

AVOID FIRE SALES

Once you understand market pricing, understand your own cost structure. What does it take for you to run your business? How much time do you need to spend selling, which therefore limits your expected revenue? How much time will you be unavailable because of other interests or vacations? On the support side, what types of services and or costs will you need to absorb to keep your practice running?

Keep in mind when you develop these estimates that no one wants to pay you more because you are sloppy at running your business. Just as you are organized to optimize your revenue, be aware that you must always keep a handle on costs—like any business.

With the market price and your own cost structure in place, you can establish your range of acceptable fees. The range, of course, reflects the type of projects you may assume because some may be inherently more valuable than others.

Once that price is set, maintain it. Don't accept work for below your market price because this practice depreciates your own value. Some consultants attempt special promotions, but keep in mind there is a truism about price: You get what you pay for.

> I used to offer free or no-cost evaluations for program/project assessments in order to present and sell to the client the benefits of engaging in my services. I found that the success rate of converting those situations to engagements was not as high as I thought they should be. So, I believed that the no-cost approach did not produce any more work than charging for upfront assessment and proposal activity. In fact, I found that as soon as I began charging for those upfront fact-finding services, I was able to convert a much higher percentage into engagements. The lesson gets back to basic value perceptions. If it doesn't cost anything, that is its value. If the client pays for it, they *will* pay attention to it. —*Dave Ellison*

PART

III

FROM THE
CLIENT'S POINT
OF VIEW

WHY NOW?

As companies clamor for employees in one of the tightest labor markets ever, the stress of recruiting the right hires has become chronic. Some executives may wonder why they should bother with this new free-agent marketplace, since what is really wanted are regular employees. Why should they fight it out in two markets—the regular hire and the consulting world—rather than concentrate their efforts on the one hiring goal?

The questions are not unrelated because the markets are not unrelated. The market for executive-level talent is so tight partly because of the number of people who have opted for an independent career. Certainly, the demographics of the aging baby boomers and the Generation X workers plays a big role; however, just as the shift of women in the labor market created a surge in the 1970s, this shift of free agents out of the universe of potential employees has an impact as well.

The obvious correlation is to the financial marketplace. A treasurer's role would be far easier if the company needed to deal only with long-term debt. But in truth, most companies use an array of financial market instruments. From term debt, lines of credit, lease financing, collateralized obligations, and marketable securities to foreign exchange futures for hedging purposes, the financial function has long exploited the diversity in the financial marketplace to optimize the needs of the enterprise for flexibility and capital access.

Human capital is much the same. There are many different "instruments" by which human capital can be deployed in an organization. Shrewd companies recognize this factor and work the markets to ensure that human capital is appropriately allocated and managed.

Companies need to focus on both the regular hire and the free-agent market concurrently in order to optimize their human capital strategies. You may not be able to find the perfect vice president of marketing quickly, but you can bring in a consultant to launch several marketing initiatives in the meantime. Put in financial terms, you are trading long-term capital for short-term financing. Similarly, an interim manager in a troublesome division may provide the data you need to be able to decide the future needs of that operation, much like a letter of credit is required to secure certain trade finance activities.

This type of labor market optimization falls into five main categories: (1) insourcing new skills, (2) accelerating time to market, (3) leveraging existing management, (4) evaluating or assessing current initiatives, and (5) providing interim management. The following sections provide some example of how companies have used spot expertise in each of these areas.

INSOURCING

Insourcing is when a company needs to bring in skills or specific content expertise that are not resident in the organization. An insourcing need often arises from a new initiative or opportunity, where the organization lacks some key element required to execute the right response. It can be functional knowledge, analytic methodologies, or specific approaches that need to be deployed by the enterprise.

A major financial services institution believed that transacting business over the Internet would be the way of the future for its small business customers. A leader in leveraging technology in banking, the company was committed to enabling its customers to harness this tremendous money-making vehicle by offering a safe, fast, and reliable way to process credit card transactions over the Internet; however, they also recognized that they didn't have all of the tools needed to provide this service properly.

The company needed to better understand its customers' priorities and needs. The only way to do that was to segment their customer base and ask specific questions. This would require substantial marketing using the bank's tried-and-true vehicle of direct mail. Using targeted mailers, they could ascertain the levels of interest and measure the receptivity of certain customer segments for Internet banking. Unfortunately, no one internally had the expertise on both the direct mail side as well as the Internet side to provide that essential information. The bank turned to M^2 to insource the right expertise to enable it to accomplish this key conversion of existing customers to a new technology channel.

Our consultant had been part of the financial and marketing team at American Express, so he was an expert in the direct mail marketing of financial services offers. He became part of a newly formed e-commerce team, which was charged with developing the appropriate tools to analyze existing customers and then create the data to identify specifically the kinds of customers (by segment, by state, by SIC code, etc.) who would be most likely to adopt the new service.

The expertise lacking internally was the facility with direct mail databases to be able to cull out the appropriate target client. This knowledge gleaned from many years at one of the preeminent users of such information was then leveraged, with the consultant using his direct mail expertise to determine the ideal direct mail key message content and to oversee the execution of the campaign to convert these clients to the Internet channel.

ACCELERATING PRODUCT/SERVICE DELIVERY

As the saying goes, time waits for no man. For many companies, critical projects need to occur at specific times whether or not the staff is on board to handle them. As such, augmenting a current and often overworked staff, with the intent of keeping key initiatives on schedule, is a typical use of the new labor market.

A rapidly growing and highly successful consulting organization, concentrating on providing new food concepts to the consumer packaged goods industry, recently started a new market research facility. As part of this effort, they needed a specialized market research consultant to assist in analyzing reporting results.

The new market research facility was located at a high traffic point in a major West Coast city, where a wide cross-section of domestic and international consumers could be "intercepted" for research. Consumers are presented with a concept, a tasting, and then asked to fill out a questionnaire consisting primarily of closed-end questions. Research takes place on Thursday through Saturday. This facility was the linchpin in a company expansion strategy. It was imperative that the initial work done here be of the highest quality because it would be the testament to the success of the endeavor.

In the interest of ensuring that the project time line was not missed, the firm wanted to add some additional analytical horsepower to its complement of skills. Results needed to be presented in topline form within approximately 48 hours of the research. An external resource was needed to oversee the entire process from tabulation to report development.

An experienced consultant who had worked with several specialty research firms was secured to champion this project to fruition. The consultant was charged with developing the research tool and then quickly tabulating and analyzing results. Final detailed reports needed to be presented two weeks following the topline. As needed, the research consultant would be involved in questionnaire development and/or client management and client presentations, depending on time commitments and client needs.

By bringing in this just-in-time research and management expertise, the firm was able to deliver the results it needed from its new facility and serve its clients in a highly responsive way. And all of it happened on time.

LEVERAGING AN EXISTING TEAM

Similar to the need to keep projects on track, there is also the need to ensure that the efforts of an ongoing team are reinforced and optimized. Often, all efforts are focused on a goal in such a concentrated way that no one notices that one ancillary area has not been addressed. Of course, that tangential omission could impede the efforts of the team. In this case, bringing in a consultant to ensure that the effort proceeds is really leveraging the existing team.

In one situation, a world leader in healthcare supplies was in the midst of a major conversion to a SAP system. This type of enterprisewide automation would enable the firm to make major leaps in productivity as well as customer service responsiveness. Two financial modules, Accounts Payable and General Ledger, had already been implemented on time and on budget. Three additional modules, Project System, Fixed Assets, and Accounts Receivable, were scheduled to convert on an aggressive timetable.

As a result of some shifts in personnel assigned to the team, the company was concerned that the project could not remain on track because a key part of the process was missing. The company wasn't prepared to provide the type of training and change management orientation that was needed to have all of the people in the organization understand how profoundly this project would shape the business. The company was not prepared to communicate the changes to the employees and get their buy-in for the new infrastructure in a timely way.

They turned to M^2 to identify an experienced change management project manager to step in and assume that critical project management role in implementing the organizational change leadership project plan for this key initiative. The organizational development expert selected was a senior executive with both line and staff management stripes, so the consultant had an affinity with the various constituencies to the change.

Our consultant had to develop a curriculum for 300 to 400 employees, which involved not only the more standard education or training but also included positive inspiration about the changes in their work that would come with the new system. The goal of the organization was to create a groundswell of support for the initiative, which required a credible, creative individual who could breathe profound impact into what might otherwise have been a dry subject. Our consultant was an accomplished organizational development practitioner with great communication skills who was able to help overcome the inevitable resistance to change with tact, understanding, and a sense of fun and humor.

For the client, this engagement was as critical as the system installation itself; in any major systems conversion, the ultimate success of the project and realization of cost savings and efficiencies depend on the users' ability and willingness to use the new methodology. Our consultant contributed critical project management support toward this goal, ensuring that the users had what they needed to succeed, and freeing the project leader to stay focused on the big picture.

ASSESSING THE SITUATION

Independent audits have been used to validate financial information, because it has become a truism that an outside eye can often discern irregularities far more quickly than an inside one. This is true not only of financial records but of various strategic and operational issues as well.

Here is one case of an outside assessment role: The business information services department of one of the largest publishers in California operated a program management office that, among other things, was responsible for ensuring that project management and cost-tracking standards were communicated and followed throughout the organization. In addition, the team also tracked high-level financial information for critical projects in order to ensure that key financial and accounting information was appropriately viewed, sorted, and analyzed for management.

The company was in the process of installing Oracle financial systems and turned to M^2 to identify a financial project manager to assist the company in assessing the current tracking process, as well as to manage the tasks necessary to successfully transition to the new tracking system. In order to achieve these goals, the consultant needed to evaluate the current information flows and tracking processes to understand whether the right information in the current environment was being captured in the best way. By performing such an assessment first, the consultant could then ensure that the new reporting structure would capture the requisite activity and data.

The consultant needed to work with the Oracle project team to understand the future system's capabilities and how they would interface with the program management office. He also had to identify the changes that would be required to work within the new system, specifically assessing how they will impact the current status-reporting process and associated procedures that company project managers were now required to report on their projects. It became clear in the early phase of the project that the assessment phase was critical because the new Oracle system represented a complete departure from the ways of the past.

A skillful financial consultant with experience in large compartmentalized organizations was engaged to tackle the project. Early on in the project, it became clear that there was resistance to the new reporting and accountability process. This stemmed in part from the fact that the new system was ushering in a new discipline into the organization. The new system, as well as the cultural changes within the organization that prompted it, required that procedures become more consistent and accurate.

Given this sensitivity, the consultant needed to work with the project managers to help them understand the importance of compliance with the new reporting methods. The final deliverable was a smooth-running program tracking department, where "smooth running" meant that the department received accurate and timely reports from all key project management teams and produced top-quality and timely reports for senior management on project costs. Utilizing the expertise of our consultant, the company realized a smooth and rapid transition to its new financial tracking system.

INTERIM MANAGEMENT

Managers depart unexpectedly all of the time, a truism that the executive search industry depends on for its very existence. In some cases, there may be an heir apparent, someone ready to step up to the challenge of a new management role. Often, however, the organization must make do until a regular hire arrives four to six months down the road. An alternative is filling the position on an interim basis, as did the client described below.

An exciting Internet directory and publishing company that was a leader in Internet navigation technology and that had attracted advertisers like Microsoft, Ford, GM, Mastercard, and AT&T was heralded as one of the top-ten sites on the Web in 1998. The firm's cofounders attracted investors and were aggressively growing the company by seeking and acquiring funding, through acquisition, and/or by consolidation/rollup. A public offering was not out of the question, and in 1998, when this situation occurred, the Internet IPO feeding frenzy had not yet unleashed its full force.

Because of the acquisition pipeline, the venture funding opportunities on the growth side, and the need to demonstrate flawless financial management in this key period, the firm needed a seasoned financial professional to provide strategic and operational advice to the company's leadership on how to grow the company by successful acquisition/merger strategy and execution.

Ultimately, the consultant also provided hands-on financial management and reporting. Through his expert financial leadership, the team was able to assuage potential investors about any concerns they may have had about the financial management of the company's newly raised capital. The client management team was able to learn from this interim expert, raising the financial expertise quotient of the entire group. On the acquisitions side, the consultant partnered with the management team to (1) evaluate the acquisitions pipeline of start-up partners (two- to three-person organizations), (2) assess the peer merger pipeline, and (3) oversee larger company merger/purchase opportunities. Our seasoned interim CFO gave the company just the right credentials and associated credibility to jump to the next level of growth and sophistication.

CASE STUDY: THE JUST-IN-TIME ANALOGY

In the 1990s, when the specter of a prolonged recession had many companies searching for new ways to reduce costs, improve margins, and maintain competitiveness, many firms looked east to the Asian economies for new ideas. One idea that is very transferable and that could have profound implications for companies of all sorts is just-in-time (JIT) inventory.

With the onslaught of Asian competition in the 1980s, American manufacturers had to make dramatic changes in their operations. One of the most far-reaching was the adoption of JIT inventory techniques. As its name suggests, JIT practices enable producers to minimize inventory by stocking only what is needed for the next day or week's production. Stocks are rebuilt as they are depleted, with regular shipments from suppliers. To ensure that no stockouts occur, vendors in many industries maintain an automated linkage with client information and/or manufacturing systems.

JIT translates directly to the bottom line because the cost of goods sold is reduced. Capital costs of holding excess inventory, as well as warehouse space and physical handling costs, are minimized. Operating efficiency is also improved because seldom-used items need not be stocked at all.

Certainly, other nonmanufacturing concerns could use JIT techniques for inventory management. But the biggest impact of the JIT concept is to apply it out of the traditional inventory setting and use it to manage a totally different type of inventory—the management staff.

Unlike production, clerical, or support staff, management staff is traditionally viewed as a fixed unit. The workload of an organization builds until it is clear that another profes-sional is needed and a new analyst or manager is hired. So the management inventory is added in chunks, as opposed to as it is needed, or just in time. Consequently, there are regular periods where the organization is understaffed and stressed or overstaffed and bloated.

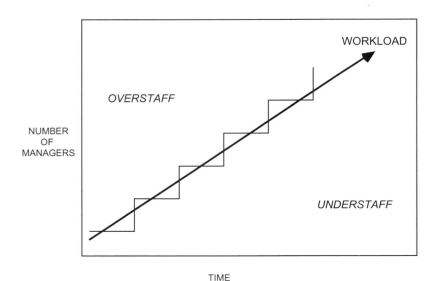

FIGURE 11–1 TRADITIONAL GROWTH IN MANAGERIAL STAFF

This situation is especially true in volatile industries where business horizons change quickly. Technology companies are notorious for a "boom-and-bust" mentality that prompts massive hiring when times are good and wholesale layoffs when the business cycle weakens. By extension, seasonal businesses seldom vary the management staff. It has long been the practice for such businesses to staff the support or nonexempt functions for the low-volume period and then backfill the peak periods with temporaries; however, few businesses consider such variable staffing in the management ranks, leading to a steady-state management level that is above the theoretical floor.

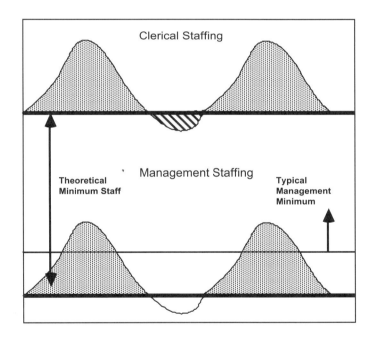

BUSINESS CYCLE

FIGURE 11–2 PEAK STAFFING MODEL

Similarly, organizations often "stock" seldom-used resources to make sure they have them when necessary. So that skill, whether it be producing the annual report or running MBA recruiting, is deployed in some other way during the rest of the year. By definition, this process is suboptimal because the fill-in work usually does not need to be performed by someone who is paid a specialist's wage.

JIT staffing could change this picture dramatically with an immediate bottom-line impact. By adding staff in the increments as it is needed, labor costs can be reduced. The excess capacity created by adding "whole bodies" is immediately eliminated when part-time resources are deployed as an alternative. This process enables companies to better match production needs with productive resources.

"Bingeing and purging" of staff can also become a thing of the past because companies could use JIT to handle volume fluctuations; businesses could acquire contract professionals as needed to handle business increases. These outside managers could be eliminated as business activity slows, enabling companies to lay off fewer actual employees. Similarly, in cyclical businesses, contract professionals can staff peak periods, allowing a company to maintain a leaner permanent professional staff.

By buying only what you need when you need it, JIT staffing would enable companies to save on specialized resources. An expert researcher, for example, would need to be deployed only for the four to six months the project takes.

JIT inventory enjoyed widespread adoption because the following factors converged:

- Competitive pressures requiring drastic measures
- Technology developments that enabled precise monitoring of stock levels and online access to suppliers
- Increased sophistication of the transportation network, allowing timely delivery of materials

Similarly, the following new developments are driving the idea of JIT staffing:

- Demographic changes creating a large pool of skilled professionals available on a project or part-time/JIT basis
- Advent of intermediaries creating efficient ways to tap this reservoir of professionals and locate the precise talents needed
- Global pressures to maintain the most competitive posture

But perhaps the biggest catalyst of JIT staffing is the nascent trend away from bureaucracy. Companies are beginning to recognize that traditional organizational structures designed by managerial scientists in prior decades are becoming outmoded. Success within the organization no longer depends on one's title or level on the organization chart; rather, success is contingent on performance and the demonstrated ability to achieve business goals.

As companies begin to organize around goals instead of a traditional bureaucracy, JIT techniques become even more appealing. Effective JIT staffing enables a company to bring together the resources it needs when it needs them; JIT staffing enables companies to develop, execute, implement, and profit from a project just in time.

CHOOSE YOUR WEAPON

TIME IS MONEY

From the client's point of view, winning the war for talent is all about making your move strategically and decisively to get that first-strike impact. In other words, the value of this new brand of expertise is time. And time is money. To get the optimal results from bringing in interim talent, a company needs to be configured to quickly identify and select just-in-time expertise.

GET IT IN THE BUDGET

Identification of who can help in a given situation pre-supposes identification of the need. As the saying goes, "Denial is not just a river in Egypt." Many companies fail to recognize issue areas until a crisis occurs.

Some problems or opportunities are spontaneous by nature; a key executive departs suddenly or a new business opportunity develops quickly and needs immediate action; however, other situations arise because management did not methodically identify a need.

One reason this happens is that people strategies are often not incorporated into business strategies. Tremendous intellectual effort is expended toward developing a thoughtful or even actionable strategic plan. Ambitious business goals are defined, but we seldom assign human resources to those deliverables.

Many years ago, in my prior life as a management consultant, we would spend weeks developing a detailed tactical plan for our recommendations; however, we never put the people to the plan and explained who might tackle these activities. Of course, there was always a portion of the project earmarked for our firm, but the other resources needed to complete an initiative weren't explicitly appointed.

In truth, for many strategic and operational tasks required of an organization, any number of human resource providers could complete the work. Consulting firms could handle certain types of analytic processes, and a specialty boutique firm could assume responsibility for a marketing research deliverable. New hires may be envisioned for parts of the plan, whereas redeployed resources are used for others. Independent consultants may be best to anchor certain efforts; however, very seldom are these resource types mapped into the business planning process.

Large pieces of work can often be handled by outside entities. From a terminology standpoint, we often distinguish between *insourcing* and *outsourcing*. Outsourcing is sending out a deliverable or chunk of work, whereas insourcing is bringing the resources in-house to accomplish the task.

Outsourcing is often more planned because it usually involves large contractual relationships, such as mailroom services, janitorial operations, or Website hosting. Insourcing, however, is rarely given appropriate attention.

Several of our larger and more progressive clients have become adept at inviting us into the business planning process so we can offer input about what types of initiatives may best be achieved by free-agent expertise. Similarly, we also gain a better appreciation for their hiring challenges, in terms of where interim management assistance may be needed. Understanding their insourcing needs enables us as a preferred broker to proactively identify interesting interim expertise for them.

Too often, this resourcing process is relegated solely to the budget process. Managers routinely "throw something in" for consultants because they may recognize that some average amount of money is magically spent on consultants each year. A better approach would be to identify the tasks to be handled by independent consultants and to price the work accordingly. When expertise can be the difference between getting to market first or last, it's surprising how seldom it's factored explicitly into the operating budget.

IDENTIFY WHAT YOU NEED

Identifying that you need to spend the money on external expertise is half the battle. Winning the war for talent requires being able to readily identify what specific talent meets your needs.

Ten years ago, the easiest way to find a consultant was to just ask a friend of a friend; everyone had his or her own Rolodex, so no one had a corner on the market, but the marketplace has changed dramatically in the past decade. Intermediaries in this independent expertise market have emerged from the consulting business, traded up from the staffing ranks, and appeared on the Internet. This change is partly the result of the recognition that all aspects of the labor force constitute a market, not just to lower ends of unskilled or semi-skilled laborers. Where there is a market, there is an opportunity to be a market-maker and/or to exploit market imperfections. Depending on their approach, each of the players in this upper echelon of expertise may be capable of being an arbitrageur in this still very fragmented high-end talent market.

Arbitrageurs can create a market in talent, understand relative price movements, and rationalize differential pricing. An arbitrageur can locate scarce resources, in part because that is its charter, to make the market. In a perfect market, rates and terms are public information that is available in real time, and goods move instantaneously. The talent market is not a mature market, but these arbitrageurs, such as consultant brokers and Internet talent sites, are destined to play a key role in perfecting the expertise market. For now, the marketplace remains imperfect; however, the arbitrageurs still fill valuable roles for companies in need of interim talent.

As discussed in Chapter 7, intermediaries can be defined by their breadth of services across functions and their vertical reach in the organization. On average, the firms serving more junior levels on a single function basis are less likely to work with you to define the needs for your project or interim engagement. Alternatively, the firms specializing in the most senior levels of talent are far more adept at developing actionable project structures. These types of firms typically have a deliverables-driven approach; they are familiar with the types of issues that can confound a successful engagement, and they work with clients to create a thorough understanding of the scope of the work and desired results from the outset.

Similarly, the Internet has two main types of resources: vendor matching sites and consultant matching sites. At vendor matching sites, you can secure the services of any type of vendor—from a window washer to a compensation designer to develop new commission structures. Sites in this category include bizbuyer.com and killerapp.com. Given the variety of disparate services offered, these sites may or may not have sufficient consultant draw.

In this situation, you would describe your need and different consultants would bid on it. You then can opt to e-mail them for more information or to continue the dialogue.

Consultant matching sites are communities for consultants where visitors can post projects. Here, the processes differ by site. Some sites automatically match consultants to your needs through a keyword search, whereas others dispatch your project description to consultants and enable the consultant to respond directly to your query. The challenge is finding the right type of talent site because some, like Acquent.com, tend to draw more artistic and creative talent, whereas others, like iNiku.com, are far more appealing to technical consultants. These various players, whether the more traditional consultant intermediaries or the Internet-based firms, provide different services in the value chain of acquiring the expertise you need.

The first step in that value chain is identifying the problem and developing a specification for the project. Although some Internet sites allow you to post a project, the presumption is that you have already been through the issues involved. "High-touch" intermediaries often develop a specification with you and/or for you. This project development process is essential because it forms the framework for securing the right consultant. We often liken project development to the blueprints for a house; you certainly wouldn't consider beginning construction without a set.

Not all interim management firms, however, focus on the definition stage. Intermediaries from the staffing world may not be adept in this consultative type of approach, being far more used to operating from more traditional job descriptions.

The second step is identifying the candidates that suit the needs of the engagement. For some players, it's an entirely computerized process, whereas others have a more active role. Many firms go beyond the consultants in their database to search specifically for a more precise skill set, but others do not.

One wild card on the Internet side is the geography screen. If you have a finite budget and did not envision travel costs, take care in specifying the geography. Many of the sites default to a geography the consultant prefers. The distinction here is when the preference is incongruent with the consultant's actual location. Although you may love to come to San Francisco when you live in Oklahoma, be sure it is clear who will be footing the bill.

Qualification is the third step, whereby a firm makes sure that the individual is a great fit for the project or interim engagement. The more traditional intermediaries, versus the Internet sites, tend to have the lead in this area because true qualification requires judgment and insight. Many of the Internet sites leave the qualification to you, providing access to résumés for you to pursue. Alternatively, some sites let the consultants qualify themselves, enabling independent experts to attest to their capabilities in the context of your needs. Although this process can be efficient, it can also be suspect because no objective third party assesses the validity of the assertions. Validating the information by reference checking then becomes a critical part of your task of assessing the expertise of the individual.

Using an intermediary or Internet source to handle these three steps theoretically leaves you with a far more qualified set of experts from which to select. Keep in mind that it is essential that you make the choice. So much of the success of an interim engagement depends on the fit, and you and your managers can make the best assessment on that front.

SCREENING

Once you have consulting candidates for your project or interim role, the task then is to select the optimal resource. Selecting a consultant is not the same as selecting an employee. In fact, it often requires an entirely different thought process. By definition, the analysis that must be done to see if the individual fits the corporate culture in the long run is irrelevant in this new expertise market. The more important question is can the person perform the task at hand—period.

At times, the task at hand requires some ancillary skills, such as good interpersonal communication skills, expertise with a given system or process, or sensitivity to certain issues. Some of these tangential elements may even have cultural fit undercurrents, and all of these dimensions are certainly fair game in the interim management screening process; however, the degree to which an independent consultant demonstrates that dimension is commensurate with the importance of that dimension to the task at hand—period.

Similarly, the traditionally functional selection criterion used for employees is often not optimal for an interim or project-oriented resource. By definition, a project manager is brought in to do something because of some complication—either there are quality problems on the line, an IPO is imminent, or a division needs to be run while a successor to the newly departed incumbent is found. That complication—the situational dimension—is most critical to the success of the engagement.

For example, a technology company needed an interim controller to sort through major system issues while the search was on for a permanent controller. Although the regular job required a CPA, supervisory experience, and facility with a certain enterprise management system, most of those attributes were not germane in the project assignment. The key evaluation criterion was: Has the consultant ever resolved this kind of mess before and in a similar scale environment? Too often, companies slight the situational dimension because they are too accustomed to the requirements for the traditional regular position.

Figure 12–1 highlights this tradeoff. Functional and industry expertise quotients are the horizontal and vertical axes, respectively. Taken alone, a company can be indifferent to individuals with a different mix of expertise; however, when adding in the situational element, represented by the circle size, the most appropriate choice becomes clear.

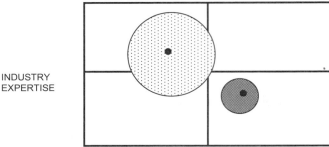

INDUSTRY
EXPERTISE

FUNCTIONAL EXPERTISE

CIRCLE SIZE IS PROPORTIONATE TO
SITUATIONAL EXPERTISE

FIGURE 12–1 THE EXPERTISE TRADEOFF

Similarly, minimum experience requirements are often not relevant in the context of outside interim and project managers. Independent consultants tend to be experienced managers; junior professionals do not have the track record to set up a successful consulting practice. For permanent jobs, especially those in professional or staff units like marketing, the seniority mix within a department is important. An overqualified individual may adversely impact morale and create succession planning and career path problems for the manager. On a project basis, however, the best option for the role might be a more senior manager. He or she can finish the project more quickly. Additionally, the right individual can add real value to an organization by helping the more junior managers in the unit. The outside expert can train these individuals in the expertise he or she was hired to provide.

In the start-up environment, external expertise can afford welcome structure and focus. The consultant charged with setting up the recruiting process or negotiating offshore packaging rights doesn't need to get caught up in the tremendous frenzy involved in getting financing. The consultant can concentrate on results while the management team leads the firm to the next stage.

In the start-up environment, consultants can also often provide some well-needed wisdom. Especially in the new economy Internet space, many rough-and-tumble entrepreneurial teams lack business wisdom acquired by experience. This mentorship potential can be very powerful.

If you need a different way to think about securing these resources, feel free to borrow a device M^2 has developed. We have distilled our criteria to four words beginning with the letter V and dubbed these guidelines "The 4 V's."

The first V is *veracity*. The fact that the consultant can really do what he or she claims is the interview step most people begin and end with. It is important to ascertain the specific skill set the consultant can deliver. Good probing questions to truly uncover expertise are ones that require a lot of description. It is not enough to claim responsibility for an increase in sales of 40 percent. The focus should be on how it was done; investigate the biggest obstacle to sales growth and how it was remediated, explore the people side of things—how were salespeople managed, what metrics were used.

There is also the lessons learned aspect. With 20/20 hindsight, what would the consultant have done differently? This probe often identifies the business maturity of the individual and the intangible value of the wisdom he or she could bring to the role.

It is also important to determine the skill set of the individual in a consulting role versus an employment role. If all of his or her expertise stems from positions as an employee, then how prepared and or capable is the individual in the role of consultant? One thing an experienced consultant brings to the table is the ability to act as an outsider and to enable organizations to move forward through problems and issues. Rookie consultants can sometimes demonstrate this skill, depending on their own background. Conversely, the nature of your need may or may not require this type of expertise in the consulting craft versus the content knowledge. If it does, then be sure to screen for it explicitly.

Versatility is another key characteristic of a good consultant. Someone who is an expert at risk management but who has spent all of his or her time with one company may not be the expert you need. Part of the value a consultant brings is the broadened perspective gained from experience with multiple organizations.

> I think one of the biggest advantages of being an outsider is that you see things with new eyes. Too often, employees do things just because they have always been done that way; another thing is that I have worked in so many environments that I have seen far more than most regular full-time employees have. —*Paul Thode*

If your business need would benefit from someone who has seen many variations of a particular problem across several companies, then be sure to screen for versatility. Screen, too, for versatility in type of companies. Someone who has always consulted with utility companies may not be effective in a start-up e-commerce business. Similarly, a consultant in venture-backed companies may be stifled in a large corporate environment.

Don't be fooled by long-term employment history in terms of versatility. Some employees can have very different experiences within the same company. We once worked with a "rookie" senior financial consultant whose last employee role was as the vice president of finance for a Fortune 200 semiconductor manufacturer. Although he had spent 20 years with the company, he had run an accounting group, coordinated a start-up operation in Indonesia, and overseen a turnaround in a *miquelladoro* (manufacturing) operation south of the border. These three key roles were all very different, requiring a variety of skill sets and interpersonal abilities, and demonstrating a broad level of expertise while operating in different cultural environments. He may have been a company man, but he had demonstrated a level of versatility exceeding what having one long-term employer would suggest.

Vigor is the third V to consider. The successful independent consultant will always need to ensure that his or her knowledge is constantly being refreshed and invigorated. The medical, legal, and accounting professions—the first of the independent practitioners—have long recognized the need for continuing education of its members. Similarly, the independent consultant must take ownership of this continuing education. Whether through certification programs, association training seminars, or diligent study of the latest trade journals, skills and knowledge must be renewed and refreshed to be valuable in the marketplace. Asking a consulting free agent how he maintains his leading edge in the field is more than fair game, it is an imperative.

> Reading, networking with others in my profession, and generally remaining as up to date as possible is a constant battle. It is easy to see the time spent in these areas as unproductive to the psyche or the bank account. I have to schedule the time as I would an appointment and just do it. —*Dan Kleinman*

Finally, *vision* is the last of the V's. An individual who has chosen a specialized field should have some concept of where that field is headed. A corollary to this concept is that the consultant should also have a sense of how his or her career may be defined in the context of that field.

An interesting analogue here is entertainment; a movie star may see the various roles assumed as bits and pieces in a collective body of work. In the aggregate, that body of work displays the craft of the performer. So, too, should a consultant have a body of work, which makes a statement about his or her career progression.

Probing for vision can be difficult depending on your familiarity with the field. A related topic in the news is often a good starting point. For example, asking a compensation expert his perspective on the salary structure in professional sports should afford a glimpse of his world view. Even if he is not a sports fan, he should have an opinion about the appropriateness or lack thereof of the prevailing structures.

Whatever process you structure, keep it consistent with your objective. You want to identify and select just-in-time expertise quickly. All too frequently, companies put consultants through arduous screening processes that defy the logic of the market. Independent expertise is a marketplace, a forum where talent will go for the prevailing price to a buyer. In the marketplace framework, the talent does not wait for a company to decide to interview him or her again— it moves on to the best opportunity. Many companies fail to recognize the time sensitivity of the market for virtual expertise. This is a larger issue, when you consider that the talent you try to secure inefficiently may go to a competitor who has set up an infrastructure to accommodate quick selection of hot interim executive talent.

THE PRICE IS RIGHT

◆ THE GAME SHOW MENTALITY

On the TV game show *The Price Is Right*, contestants vie for prizes based on the accuracy of their guesses about the retail purchase price of certain consumer and household goods. Whoever is the closest, without going over, wins the refrigerator, exercise bike, or stereo system. The successful contestant is the individual who is most familiar with current prices, reinforcing the notion that it does pay to go shopping.

This situation is somewhat true in the market for consulting services as well. The more you know about the goods on the shelf and their prevailing market price, the better you will fare. The most common mistake made by companies is assuming that the consulting fee is comparable to the employment cost. The thinking goes like this: "I could get someone like this for $100,000 annually, there are 2,000 hours in a year, so this person must go for $50 per hour."

Each phrase of this argument contains a salient flaw. The first is the idea that this externally oriented resource who has potentially seen and worked with more types of companies than anyone on your staff would possibly work for any compensation number you suggest. In economic terms, this is *not* a substitute product.

> Consulting has enabled me to gain a greater breadth and depth personally and professionally than any other aspect of my life . . . and certainly much more than I could ever gain in several lifetimes of full-time employment. —*Whitney Vosburgh*

Consultants like this one wouldn't consider your job, at least not at any salary you would be willing to proffer; however, if they did consider your regular role, they would probably be worth more than your typical applicant.

Second, 2,000 hours in a year is true of employees. For consultants, the relevant comparison is their billable hours. As we have already discussed, they need to have time to sell and time to stay current with developments in their field. As such, some fraction of their time is continually unavailable. This means there must be a premium on the remaining time to make up that difference. In other words, they need to gross up their straight hourly fee in order to recapture their lost time.

A related error in that statement is that it would take an external resource a comparable amount of time as an employee. Consultants as outsiders are often able to get to the heart of the matter more quickly. Often, they are freed from the "time sinks" of company meetings and have the luxury to focus only on the task at hand.

> In one job I did, we had to estimate the cost of major company projects. The client said to use a 70 percent efficiency rate for employees and 100 percent for contractors. And this was not the difference for cost of employees and benefits we were talking about. It was real productivity. —*Stephen Austin*

Finally, the statement that the consultant must therefore "go" for $X per hour is assigning a value to the person, not the work. The content of the project should define its market price. Valuing the content is often best done by valuing the impact of inaction. What would be the cost—real or opportunity—of not proceeding with the engagement? Would it mean losing a quarter's worth of revenue to the competition? Would it mean a failing division would continue to hemorrhage profits without leadership?

Another maxim of pricing is also true: You get what you pay for. Buying a world-class e-commerce strategist for $350 per hour may be a hefty price tag, but the pure expert may be able to achieve the desired result in less time than may an analyst at $125 per hour. Many clients can be penny-wise and pound-foolish.

Working with intermediaries like M^2 is one way you can gauge the market price. These firms work with so many types of projects and consultants that they have a sense of where the market is in terms of pricing. Like that shopper on *The Price Is Right*, they spend so much time in the store that they know the answers.

PRICING VARIABLES

Many variables impact the price of an engagement, some of which have little to do with the work. When negotiating prices, don't lose sight of the human across the table. If the consultant is acting as a free agent in order to maximize his or her income, then fees are the most important factor. Alternatively, if the consultant wants to maximize his or her free time, then flexibility in terms of hours and deliverables may have a currency that is far more powerful than cash. In the dot.com world of stock options, many consultants are attracted by the opportunity to get their own piece of the action.

Key aspects of the work that do impact fee structures include the following:

- *Managing people commands a premium.* This is especially true if great dysfunction exists within the organization. By extension, if you are looking for an interim executive to come in and evaluate a team and eliminate the nonperformers, then that type of decisive action demands appropriate rewards.

- *Utter chaos or absolute tedium may require hazard pay.* This pricing principle is somewhat counterintuitive. Some consulting engagements are insourced precisely because no one internally would take them on. One example we had was with a multistate hospital system that had used the incorrect tax tables to calculate the final W-2s for every employee in each of the 11 hospitals in five states. A very solid controller with good payroll and tax accounting experience could have done this in a snap; however, the task was so tedious and fraught with internal politics (i.e., eleven CEOs complaining about the accuracy of their paystubs) that no one wanted to do it. Hazard pay was warranted—and was received.

- *Some degree of glamour means a discount.* "Sexy" clients or very interesting projects often have an intrinsic value that enables a consultant to lower standard fees. Even with the long commute outside of the San Francisco city limits, we always found many interested consultants for relatively low-fee projects at Lucas Films. Being out at Skywalker Ranch was a form of compensation in and of itself. Similarly, in the early days of the Internet, many consultants would charge reduced fees for entree to e-consulting opportunities. In this way, they could build their repertoire of skills and make themselves more marketable in the long run.

- *Travel is a wildcard.* Some consultants enjoy the opportunity to be in an exotic location, so they may reduce fees for a long project in South Africa, for example. Others may balk at being asked to go to the Ozarks in the blistering heat of the summer. Travel as a factor in negotiations can swing fees either way.

- *Long-term fees are lower than short-term fees.* Good consultants should have a fee range for short projects that differs substantially from longer ones. A longer project enables the consultant to cover some of his or her unbillable time; less time is needed to be spent marketing if you know you have eight months of solid fee income. Similarly, a random one-month project may need to command a far higher price.

The best way to determine the price variables is to discuss them honestly with any consultant you want to engage. Understand from your resource what the hinge factors in the pricing equation may be, and negotiate accordingly.

DON'T FORGET THE TERMS

Although many people overlook them, contractual terms can be a big factor in negotiating the optimal price. Some consultants prefer anywhere from 25 to 50 percent of the fees paid in advance. If you have done your homework on the assessment front, this shouldn't pose a problem.

Flexibility in the time commitment can be a big factor as well. The ability for the executive to work off-site is often highly valued. Similarly, the ability to spend some time marketing for future engagements is absolutely essential for others.

Finally, there is the upside piece. Especially in the technology sector, many consultants are intent on getting a "piece of the action." Unlike potential employees who you may need to woo with large option packages, the shrewdest consultants are happy with smaller allocations. Their play, much like a portfolio manager, is diversification. They know that many of the start-ups with which they consult may not make an enormous score in the public markets; however, by taking a little slice from various companies, the odds are good that they will enjoy some upside. They play the role of venture capitalist using their own human capital as the investment consideration.

14

THE RACE IS ON

JUST DO IT

The new economy of today is all about speed. Business is done at a whole new pace, which means the deployment of this new brand of expertise has to be in sync with the speed of business.

Once you have selected the right talent and set an appropriate market price, the trick then is to make it all happen. The first obstacle for some companies is the nature of the engagement contract that is drawn up to cover the work. Far too many companies have blanket temporary staffing contracts and/or purchasing agreements, which are inappropriate for knowledge transactions.

Moreover, the contract execution process in many companies is highly time consuming. Most large companies have standard contracting agreements in excess of ten pages, which are designed to work for plumbing contractors as well as the consultant designing the annual report. The legal review for the independent consultant can be onerous.

Similarly, the insurance coverages required of the consultant are often inappropriate to the management task to be done. Again, this often stems from the fact that these agreements are meant for all contractors, not just management-level consultants. This type of red tape only draws out the process and diminishes the time value of virtual expertise.

This isn't to say that a company should not have a formalized contractual agreement with any vendor—whether company or consultant—from whom services are provided. Rather, it is to suggest that many companies could benefit by reviewing their contracting procedure to make it as expedient as possible while affording the appropriate level of protection. Specific consulting agreements addressing roles, responsibilities, intellectual property, nondisclosure, and liability issues can be quite effective.

In terms of roles and responsibilities, a consulting contract needs to specify the independent nature of the relationship, clearly defining that the consultant is not your employee and, as such, has no rights to the benefits typically accorded to employees. It should also specify that given the independent nature of the relationship, your company will not be responsible for tax withholding.

Responsibilities should be laid out as discretely as possible. Specific deliverables should be defined and described. If the deliverable is a recommendation of some sort, then clarify in what way it will be delivered. Similarly, if the consultant is supposed to orchestrate a product launch, then document what the definition of completion of that initiative will be. By extension, if you want the working papers, raw data, or any other kind of derivative documentation, then specify this requirement as well. You need to be as clear as possible about what defines fulfillment of the consultant's obligation to perform under the agreement and at what point the consultant can conclude his or her work; you don't want the consultant to say the project is over if you haven't received the value specified.

Intellectual property issues and nondisclosures go hand in hand. As we discussed in Chapter 9, in a work-for-hire agreement it is clear that the buyer owns the resultant product and any intellectual property associated with it. If this is your goal, then be sure to define the engagement as a work for hire. Alternatively, specify your intellectual property rights and/or the understanding of how such rights will be treated.

A nondisclosure agreement (NDA) works best if it is *very* clear what information cannot be disclosed. When dealing in the knowledge marketplace, care must be taken not to constrain the consultant's future project and associated income potential. We have seen many consultants walk away from engagements where the NDA was too onerous, foreclosing far too many options for the consultant's future business.

Liability is an area often dealt with by requiring certain insurance coverages. Be aware that certain types of insurance are virtually impossible for an independent consultant to obtain. Workers' compensation, by definition, requires an employer, so any independent consultant set up as an unincorporated sole practitioner will not be able to purchase workers' compensation. General liability coverage is only appropriate for those consultants with commercial office space. In some cases, consultants with home offices can take out a special rider on their homeowner's policies to satisfy this requirement. This can be expensive, however, and when you decompose the issue to its inherent risk, it is nonsensical; such liability coverage assumes that if consultants are injured walking through their own office (since in the client's workplace, the client's liability coverage is the applicable remedy), they will sue themselves. Nonetheless, we have seen consultants take out these expensive riders on homeowner's policies in order to satisfy such insurance provisions.

The bottom line is, don't just define the insurance coverages you desire; define the risks you see and the ones that seem appropriate to mitigate. One legitimate risk in knowledge work is that the consultant will not complete the engagement correctly. Errors and Omissions (E&O) insurance covers this type of risk.

E&O insurance is becoming far more available in the independent consulting world. M^2, as well as other intermediaries, offers highly discounted policies to its network of consultants. Although it is not unreasonable to require a consultant to carry E&O, for those who may not have it, the lead time can be significant. These policies are underwritten by a variety of risk classes that may or may not suit the practice of a given consultant. As such, for those who do not fit cleanly into a certain known, risk-weighted, consulting category, the underwriting must be individually tailored, and this process invariably takes time.

Finally, the other aspect of liability regards disputes and the resolution of disputes. Because litigation is so protracted today, specifying arbitration or mediation as a process of choice can reduce potential litigation costs.

THE INSIDE JOB

Once the contract is negotiated, the challenge is to get the most out of your consultant quickly. This requires a host of logistical and organizational preparations that are sometimes overlooked for independent consultants. Typically, these details are far more important in large corporations, where it is easy for an individual to become lost in the bowels of the organization. The company should have a checklist of things to be done before the consultant even arrives, including (but not limited to) the following:

- Finding a desk or hoteling station
- Getting a phone line

- Getting an equipped computer, modem, and Internet access, if needed
- Ordering/securing keys, badges, passes, etc.
- Providing hook-up to voicemail if needed
- Notifying receptionists, secretaries, the mailroom, travel departments, and security
- Creating online system hookups and passwords
- Generating a current e-mail list
- Notifying accounts payable to set up a new vendor

Failure to make such logistical arrangements can impact the success of a project and cost the company more by extending the length of the engagement. Several years ago, we saw firsthand how a routine oversight jeopardized a critical, strategic project.

A major global law firm contacted us for a senior services marketing consultant to evaluate the impact of practice-driven marketing. Our marketing executive was frustrated by the lack of response to a competitive survey she launched as an essential precursor to the project. She had been calling all of the firm's biggest and best customers; however, few of these calls were returned. The client had done a good job of communicating the project, or so she thought.

In actuality, although she had a phone, a desk, and secretarial support, the reception team had never been informed of her arrival and name. When calls came in for her, they merely informed the caller there was no one there by that name, and consequently, no record of the message was taken. Not until many phone calls had come in directed to the consultant from the survey respondents did one of the receptionists notice the trend and pause to find out if someone by that name was indeed working for the firm. By that time, so many calls had been lost that the project had to be entirely redefined, so as not to anger valued customers of the firm.

Organizational orientations should be similar to those provided to new managers; however, in addition to the normal organizational chart and company history, the consultant should be oriented to the informal organization. Providing company biographies or a brief introduction to the individuals with whom the consultant will be interfacing is one way to achieve this goal. Annotating an organizational chart with the interpersonal attributes of "who's who" is another.

This kind of organizational review is especially important for human resources managers on interim project engagements. Because they are constantly dealing with the people of the organization, they need to know what manager always complains about his staff and what manager never complains until a lawsuit is pending. This type of interpersonal introduction can save much time for the interim manager.

What many people forget is that in many cases the organization needs an orientation to the consultant as well. Restructuring paranoia takes over in many companies undergoing organizational or directional changes. Management and staff both are often leery of outsiders and fearful that their jobs will be on the line. This distrust is aggravated by the perception that these consultants are unduly compensated. They compare the $150 per hour of the consultant with their own salary, never taking into account the explicit tradeoffs involved in the roles, like the value of benefits and the cost of maintaining a consulting practice.

The project and the consultant should be introduced to any units impacted by the effort. The origins, goals, and expected results should be explained. Preferably, the consultant should present his or her methodology and solicit from the start the support and buy-in of the project from the rest of the organization. It should be made very clear that he or she has no claims on any individual's job. If a meeting cannot be convened on the subject, then a memo should be sent to all parties concerned.

These steps can be difficult in situations where an individual is brought in to evaluate organizational effectiveness with the goal of potentially reducing staff or eliminating certain business lines. The client and consultant should jointly strategize the way in which this information will be presented to the rank and file of the organization. Alternatively, in some situations it takes an outsider to be able to fully assess the undercurrents in an organization.

> An employee, particularly in the organizational development/behavior arena, cannot do most of what I do as effectively as I can. Trust is a critical component of what I do; with me, an employee or manager can say what they really feel, recommend what they feel makes the most sense, and be assured that it won't come back to haunt them. —*Barry Deutsch*

Similarly, clients and vendors should be informed as necessary. An interim manager filling in for a sales manager on leave should be introduced to clients in advance and, in many cases, subsequently in person. This process actually presents a wonderful opportunity to reconnect with customers and demonstrate your commitment to customer service.

Organizational barriers often block the success of a project. Besides the distrust factor, there is the larger issue of the lack of familiarity and training for managers about how to manage outside experts. Often, they are trained and taught about managing employees without attention to the nuances of dealing with service providers. As such, traditional motivational structures are inappropriate for the independent expert. The reward for the consultant is expanding his or her client and skill base and enhancing his or her professional reputation.

This isn't to say that bonus-oriented incentives can't be created. Many independent consultants will structure contract fees that vary with performance. This arrangement is especially true in projects or interim assignments where results can be clearly and objectively assessed by error rates, financial measures, volume, or revenue growth targets. Many consultants, especially those who serve emerging-growth fields, will consider compensation in terms of options, nonliquid equity, or other in-kind payments; however, few consultants will work solely for equity because of the tax implications. The minimum cash payment, therefore, becomes the estimated tax liability of the maximum value of the equity—noncash compensation—award.

Additionally, managers should recognize the legal implications of managing outside consultants. They should be familiar with the 20 rules of the IRS regarding independent contractors. Taken individually, any one rule may be relaxed; however, the totality of the consulting engagement will determine whether the consultant is actually an employee of the company. See Chapter 8 for more information on this issue.

Take steps to ensure that managers throughout the company understand the liability issues associated with this type of knowledge resource; an engagement can start out cleanly but degrade into a classification problem, because a line manager treats an independent contractor like an employee. Failure to differentiate between different types of workers, even when done in ignorance, can create problems. The line must know the law. Some of the salient points for companies to keep in mind include the following:

- Independent consultants are free to set their own hours; as few rules as possible relative to hours worked in a day should be set.

- Consultants should be free to work from their own offices; companies may want to avoid explicit requirements for on-site execution of the project, except where necessary for security or data access reasons.

- Consultants should be free to select their own subcontractors. Clients can make recommendations but should not require a consultant to use particular subcontractors.

- Consultants should be free to offer services to the community at large. Therefore, exclusive contracts may be risky. Consultants should not be precluded from serving other clients during the life of an engagement.

Beyond the legal implications are the project management ones. Corporate managers of outside consultants must have a solid foundation in project management; in order to evaluate the expert's performance on the project, the client must understand the process. He or she must be well versed in the expected deliverables, intermediate goals, and required reports, timetable, and budget. Clients must be able to evaluate the success of an outside expert not only in terms of whether the job was completed, but also in terms of whether value was received for the money spent. Value can only be evaluated with a full understanding of the costs and the expected outcomes.

Therefore, any project, regardless of how small or routine, should have well-articulated goals and deliverables. Goals may be in terms of time frames, productivity measures, financial controls, revenue increases, client calls, and so forth. Subjective measures should be avoided. A goal for "better customer service" should be translated into a measurable one, such as a reduction in customer service complaints by 20 percent at the end of a given period.

When developing the measures, keep in mind that they also must be within the scope of the project and within the consultant's domain. A quality consultant can recommend changes to reduce inventory shrinkage; however, if those recommendations are never acted upon, then it is not the consultant's performance or recommendations that have failed.

Taking this approach toward managing consulting engagements not only makes for a more defensible and measurable final product, but it also builds the skills of the managers running the project. This is especially critical in the current business climate where no job is secure. Managers owe it to themselves and their staff to build a strong project management discipline. By doing this, corporate managers are in the process of reinventing their own skills, preparing for the day when perhaps they become external consultants.

KNOWLEDGE MANAGEMENT

Perhaps the largest issue facing companies using the new brand of expertise is ensuring the institutionalization of that knowledge once the project is concluded and the expert has gone onto new engagements. Without a mechanism to ensure retention, the company is merely a sieve into which knowledge flows in and out again; rather, it must be a reservoir that captures the flow of expertise and stores it for future use.

The best way to enable retention is to make it part of the contract with the consultant. He or she must be able to turn over the baton to an employee; the consultant must train someone in the organization on his or her approach, constructs, and activities. Someone in the organization must be left aware of potential issues remaining from the course of the project or that could arise in the future. This should be a formal requirement; for example, a product-costing project would not be considered complete until a manager is trained on the model and all associated documentation is provided.

Beyond these types of training requirements, managers must become sensitive to expertise networks. As success in an organization becomes more dependent on project management performance, those who are best able to rapidly deploy expertise will be those most recognized and rewarded. Managers must be able to rapidly identify individuals with expertise in disciplines that may be useful in the future. They must actively and deliberately develop formal and informal expertise networks, so that when the time arises they know where the knowledge may be found. This can be as simple as creating a list of individual consultants and intermediaries to call on when the need arises, or as complicated as cataloguing in a specialized database the skills of consultants used and/or considered for projects.

In larger, more established organizations, this thinking represents a profound change for many human resource managers. Increasingly, line managers will look to them to provide direction for where certain knowledge can be found. Human resources managers must become the repositories of this knowledge, proactively becoming aware of ways to secure specific expertise.

Additionally, there is the whole arena of inside consultants in addition to outside consultants. Often, especially in large organizations, the expertise may lie somewhere in the corporation. Human resources management must develop the skill matrices to understand how to tap the functional, industry, situational, and client-oriented expertise resident within the company. It must be a dynamic system that can capture the skill reinvention occurring within the organization. Not only must they develop a way to catalogue this information, but they must also create the enabling organizational structures to deploy inside experts. They must create project-centered job descriptions for key employees, which release them for special projects while maintaining or strengthening career goals.

Chapter 15

FUTURE IMPERFECT

FROM A CHAOTIC PRESENT

Most executives, even CFOs, regard a forecast, especially a sales forecast, as at best an estimate of the most likely outcome. As tribes of market analysts have discovered, nothing is more certain to diverge from the expected than an extrapolation of current trends. Why? Because probably, most trend lines are part of a much larger, more complex fluctuating cycle.

Perhaps the source of the cycle, like the source of the wave swell crashing on the beach, is economically unknowable. And if we could identify the next potentially chaotic event that would trigger the next directional change in the trend, then perhaps the very fact of having identified it would work to change the outcome. Heisenberg rules.

TO A SMOOTH FUTURE

A white-water rafter does not need a forecast of the shape and weight of every thrusting wave to be able to negotiate class IV rapids. She relies instead on her skill to be able to adroitly steer the craft through the turbulent waters. She also needs the acquired skills of anticipation and control in order to interpret effectively the meaning of each signal the churning water sends.

In writing this book, I have tried to be your white-water guide, providing the information on the rapids and the rocks ahead, as well as the state of the water as I see it. So, let's look farther down the river. What signals is the market sending us about the future for this new brand of expertise?

IT'S THE END OF A GENERATION

As I said in the early chapters, interim management 20 years ago was an oxymoron. In the intervening decades, firms like M^2 have made a market in talent. They have made such progress in advancing this notion of just-in-time expertise that Internet sites have been built to exploit the new marketplace. In the course of these developments, we have grown our future customers.

Ten years ago, when I called on a vice president of marketing, it was an educational sale; slowly, my prospects became sold on the notion of just-in-time expertise. What I didn't realize at the time was that, by default, I was also calling on the entire marketing department. As a change agent consultant came into the organization, completed a task, and left, not only was the client impressed, but so were the other incumbents. In time, those marketing staffers would rise to positions of higher authority in that client organization or others, and for them, the value of independent consulting talent no longer needed to be proven.

Traditional marketers would say that we have just been through the early adopter phase of a product/service lifecycle, and now we are into the growth phase. Now our clients are the second generation of buyers. When the decision makers are the fourth or fifth generation of buyers, we'll reach lifecycle maturity, but we have a long way to go yet.

ANY LEGAL CLARIFICATION IS GOOD

As we discussed in Chapter 8, tremendous legal ambiguity exists about the status of consultants and their right to be paid as independent workers. The independent contractor versus employee debate has raged throughout the country until even mighty Microsoft was felled by inappropriate classification of employees.

If left unresolved—which it will be until at least the end of 2001, given the election year dimension of 2000—the independent expertise trend will continue to grow. There will be pockets where growth will be stanched, like certain high-tech companies undergoing the scrutiny of the IRS or state employment regulators.

If the matter is clarified such that there is more opportunity for independent experts to be deployed without fear of running afoul of the law, then usage patterns should increase. Companies that would have loved to use an independent consultant but were fearful of the wrath of the IRS would now be new market entrants.

On that note, a bill currently under consideration in the U.S. Senate (#344, The Independent Contractor Simplification and Relief Act introduced in February 1999) will clarify the issue somewhat to the benefit of independent contractors of any kind, not just the knowledge variety. That bill has been tabled as of this writing, but it is anticipated that it may be resurrected in early 2001.

Conversely, although it may sound paradoxical, retrenchment of the law may afford greater opportunities. If future political developments produce legislation that tightens up the regulation of employment, then in the interests of employee protection and security of tenure, the likely reaction is for employers to seek ways to avoid the commitments inherent in employment contracts. If we look internationally, such a directional shift recently occurred in Holland, and this resulted in an uptick in interim management usage.

REENGINEERING BY ANY OTHER NAME . . .

A large company might be compared to a large engine: the bigger it becomes, the more complex the problem of control and the larger the proportion of its motive power that needs to be devoted to control mechanisms, to the detriment of its power-to-weight ratio. Information technology has provided the framework for the control mechanisms in the modern enterprise and is, therefore, a principal agent of the transformation of the corporation.

Call it downsizing, rightsizing, process redesign, or reengineering, the trend toward modifying the structure of an organization to rationalize the way information is collected, shared, and deployed has become a fact of life. In many cases, reengineering was not seen so much as a path to become more effective as it was a necessary survival mechanism when margins came under irresistible pressure. Have we arrived at the end of this path? Might companies begin to regret the amount of sheer intellectual horsepower and capability that may have been jettisoned in the name of corporate competitiveness?

Perhaps the rate of change will slow, but there is certainly no reversal foreseeable in the near term. Any industry where human capital is the largest single economic cost will come under significant competitive pressure to reduce its cost of capital. In this situation, the need for change is continuous, but the effect of change tends to be sudden and chaotic, like an earthquake that relieves the built-up pressure and tensions in the earth's crust.

In his books, Professor Charles Handy outlines his famous "shamrock" model of the future shape of successful organizations. Like a shamrock, an organization would have three leaves. One leaf is the core of regular employees, a universe that would be somewhat different from its historical composition. That core would comprise, on average, younger workers working longer hours. They are paying their dues, so to speak. A second leaf comprises outsourced services, like the mailroom and the janitorial staff. Finally, the third leaf comprises teams of temporary managers, a.k.a. consultants, and temporary staff members who are assembled to contribute to particular projects, then dismantled and reassembled again with different constituencies to achieve different goals.

Moreover, Handy posits, most of the value of the organization will come from those noncore employee leaves because they represent highly skilled knowledge workers. Not only will they be highly skilled, but they will also be highly paid, as befits their skill level.

For those who have difficulty envisioning the shamrocked organization, Handy offers a perfect, albeit counterintuitive analogy, the British Army. Many men enter the British Army with the understanding that they will be well fed, clothed, and most important, superbly trained during their period of service. At certain key points, it is expected that many of them will leave the military service; there is only room for so many colonels, and eventually generals, after all. Those who leave are not disgraced in any way, in fact, quite the contrary. The training afforded by the military stint is viewed favorably in other career situations by prospective employers who understand this logical progression.

The enterprise, then, is like the army. You go in early, work long and hard with the full understanding that some people will leave because only few can stay, and progress upward through the ranks.

Looking at Handy's shamrock model through the lens of reality, no one knows if there is an ideal balance between the relative weight of the three elements. That said, it is obvious that an organization that can learn to cultivate the fluid and flexible mode of the shamrock will be better equipped to manage through periods of chaotic change.

Notice, however, that as an organization moves along the continuum from total bureaucratic integration toward total flexibility—that is, becoming more shamrock-like or more virtual—two demands become more critical: (1) total commitment to interpreting customer needs and satisfaction and (2) an intense involvement in quality and quality control, especially in terms of those components that are being supplied by outside vendors.

It seems likely, therefore, that experience with customer care and operational quality will become skills likely to be retained by companies. In Handy's terms, these would become core competencies. Alternatively, those workers with significant depth in those areas will find their knowledge to be of great worth in the talent market.

Potentially, the dot.com phenomenon is at least anecdotal evidence of the evolution of the shamrock notion. The core employees tend to be young and impassioned. They work frightfully long hours, and many burn out and leave. Meanwhile, in the interest of speed, the companies outsource many services, and they insource quite a bit of expertise. The dot.coms may not know that not only are they reshaping the way business is done, but they may also be indicative of a whole new organizational model.

THE SECURITIZATION OF HUMAN CAPITAL

As the new organizational models begin to take hold and the free-agent expert becomes an expected part of a staffing equation, the market for talent will mature. Right now, it is still fragmented, despite the efforts of the Internet entities. With time will come maturation.

Again, the interesting analogy is the financial marketplace. As the financial markets became more mature, new levels of sophistication were reached. Complex instruments were developed to meet the needs of clients. Swaps, collars, and caps became regular tools of financial officers, and the most astute investment bankers began securitizing assets, everything from mortgages to car loans. The common thread in the race to securitize is that the asset bears an income stream; a mortgage has a coupon payment, as does a loan. To minimize risk that an individual loan may become delinquent or could potentially prepay, large pools of payments were aggregated to enable a predictable cash flow to underpin the bond.

In February 1997, a new financial instrument hit the market, David Bowie Bonds. David Bowie, the British rock star, issued bonds that were backed by future royalty payments on his music. The $55-million issue of ten-year notes was bought in entirety by Prudential Insurance Co. of America. Moody's Investors Service rated the notes single-A-3, which is a superior rating for a new type of instrument. As Bloomberg, the financial news service, reported at the time:

> This is the latest twist in the asset-backed bond market, which last year grew to a record $165 billion. By selling the bonds, Bowie gets ready access to cash, instead of waiting for future roy-alties to come in. "I wish all our clients were as innovative as David Bowie," said David Pullman, managing director at Fahnestock & Co., which arranged the private sale. "David's ability to embrace new ideas is a testament to his position as a living rock legend."

So what do rock-and-roll bonds have to do with the new brand of expertise? The Bowie Bonds represent the first step in securitization of human capital. In truth, there is a tangible asset—royalty income—aggregated from many payees, the various royalty streams from all of the licensed intellectual property. But underlying that asset is the rock-and-roll legend himself. Isn't it fair to assume that business legends could create the same type of market structure?

An excellent consultant should be able to command strong fees for a foreseeable long-term horizon. By extension, 500 accomplished consultants would have a similar income stream. By aggregating the fees of a pool of consultants, you could offset any irregularities in the income streams due to slow periods, extended European vacations, or lost time because of illness.

Consultants, who would be the issuers of the security, would be interested in this type of financial structure because it would smooth out their cashflow cycles; no longer would they need to plan vacation periods for six months to one year in advance. Also, the income security gained would not be at the expense of independence. Moreover, as the value of the knowledge reflected in the bond pool increased, payment flows would increase as well.

The market would value this bond because it prices knowledge. In boardrooms everywhere, companies are trying to understand how to value intellectual assets. GAAP (generally accepted accounting principles) accountants are grappling with new ways to account for intellectual assets on balance sheets. Patent-rich companies, like Dow Chemical, are launching initiatives to thoroughly catalogue discrete intellectual assets and their patents, and to develop plans to generate revenue by licensing unused properties. A consultant bond would place a value on knowledge, on human capital.

Taking this idea even further, one can look at how sophisticated the securitization of mortgages has become today. Where once Fannie Mae consolidated a pool of conventional mortgages only, now secondary marketers are selling all sorts of mortgages. In some cases, they are selling "story bonds," where the mortgages may be entirely on resort properties. In essence, the marketers are differentiating the assets in the aggregated pool.

This differentiation could happen in the consultant bond market as well. There could be marketing consultant bonds and human resources consultant bonds. If the former became heavily weighted with a very high-profile type of expertise (e.g., today's e-commerce), then chances are good that the security value would rise. Similarly, scarce resources could impact the pricing and reflect the true market price of talent.

In the end, the securitization of human capital would relieve some of the barriers to people becoming free agents because income stability is improved for the consultant without sacrificing independence.

THE GENIE IS OUT OF THE BOTTLE

Finally, the prospects for the independent consulting market are bright, simply because it's happening now. As I was researching this topic with the consultants in the M^2 network, I was continually amazed and gratified to hear the passion with which these impressive individuals describe their career choices. Most of these people won't go back to an employed life with all of the restrictions that may impose. If they do, it would be only for a short stint.

In 1998, our venture capital clients were pushing us to add a search service for full-time employees to our product line. We were reluctant because we knew we were representing individuals who had established a consultancy—they had made a discrete choice.

To validate our assumption, we asked a group of consultants who were attending a luncheon. The answer was astounding. Would they take a permanent job? "Maybe," was the reply. If the opportunity was worth it, it may be considered. As one consultant put it, "What does it matter anyway . . . What is a job after all? . . . This would just be a two-year gig."

So consultants today see their careers as a continuum, where they will go from consultant to employee to consultant again. They make that transition because they will be armed with new, marketable skills.

> A month ago, I accepted a position as General Manager for an Internet, e-business company. This was a conscious decision to broaden and update my skills to meet the new business climate. I decided that if I could understand the new business paradigm, I would again have skills that would make me desirable to clients. I expect to utilize these down the road when I am either on my own or building a new consulting practice. —*Margery Mayer*

So, the genie is out of the bottle, and it can't be put back in. The option to work independently at chosen intervals is too powerful a lure. The new brand of expertise is here to stay.

APPENDIX

PROFILES OF QUOTED CONSULTANTS

David Potter, Warwick, MA

David is a versatile, results-focused executive with a record of success in entrepreneurial and turnaround management consulting with intellectual property, consumer products and financial services companies. He also has line experience in general management and marketing. He has demonstrated success in planning and managing new ventures and marketing programs at Fortune 100 companies, start-ups, and early growth companies across a range of industries. He was a core member of a team that built one of the insurance industry's most profitable long-term care divisions. He also created a new marketing organization that proved to be instrumental in the turnaround of a consumer products company.

Sandy Di Nubilo, Redwood City, CA

Sandy is a Human Resources executive with a well established and successful track record in administrative maagement functions, recruiting, compensation/benefits analysis, facilities planning, employee relations, strategic planning, and organizational development. Her unique area of expertise is working with start-up companies that may be impeded by a lack of professional environment, and helping them evolve to a professional level by building management teams to achieve true success. Her clients include many pre-IPO companies that need solid HR wisdom in their growing enterprises.

Barry Deutsch, Manhattan Beach, CA

Since 1970, Barry has been helping small, medium, and large businesses transform change into a competitive advantage, create measurable performance improvement, and in the process, keep on track. Based in California for nearly 30 years, he has had the opportunity to apply organization and management development expertise to some of the state's most well known technical firms, such as General Dynamics, Logicon, Magnavox Research Laboratories, McDonnell Douglas, Motorola, North American Philips, Northrop, and Pertec.

Stephanie Carhee, Pittsburgh, CA

A professional and well-seasoned marketing expert and event planner Stephanie's experiences include collateral development, program development, project management, strategic marketing, brand management, and trade show management. Her expertise is in vendor management, including negotiation of vendor contracts and pricing scales, identification of new vendors, budget management, facilitation of project update meetings, management of marketing and product data in support of the selling process, master schedule development, and overall progress and results presentation.

Dana Free, Redwood Shores, CA

Dana is a seasoned sales and marketing professional with specific expertise in the call center arena. Dana has been responsible for training in state-of-the-art B2B and B2C tele-businesses; coaching and mentoring telebusiness agents, supervisors, and managers; creating online scripts, call guides, and sales force automation (SFA) applications; and fueling continuous improvement processes in self-directed teams. Dana has created telebusiness teams and has served on the board of the Northern California American Telebusiness Association. He has intimate knowledge of customer relationship management (CRM) applications as a result of representing Kanisa, an e-Service Portal, to Global 200 clients.

Janet Birgenheier, Fairfax, CA

Janet has an extensive background in developing training programs for financial services organizations, including Citicorp, Bank of America, Wells Fargo, and Charles Schwab. These programs include self-paced instructional workbooks, online seminars, and live, stand-up training programs. She is extremely well versed in a wide range of financial products, including asset-based finance, private banking, retail banking, and investment products. Her training expertise includes needs assessment, design, development, delivery, and post-evaluation. She has seven years of experience as an employee benefit communication and training consultant with Towers Perrin, Watson Wyatt, and Kwasha Lipton. During this part of her career, she developed numerous stock options, 401(K), and deferred compensation campaigns to inform and educate employees.

Lynn Astalos, Los Gatos, CA

Lynn developed a product and technology launch program for Cisco System's load balancing technology, acting as the interface between product development, product management, and marketing staffs for a virtual team spread across the country. He managed dozens of product launches for start-ups and Fortune 500 companies in various high-tech industries, managing cross-functional teams to develop strategic positioning and tactical go-to-market plans. He was recently engaged by Hewlett-Packard to launch e-business services through HP's Commerce for the Millennium subsidiary for small businesses in Canada. He has 16 years of experience as a generalist in marketing, including five years at General Motors (corporate PR) and eight years at Applied Materials (corporate communications). Also, he was born and raised in Tokyo, speaks native Japanese, and has traveled extensively throughout Asia.

Carole Rehbock, Berkeley, CA

Since 1988, Carole has had her own firm, Consulting and Coaching Solutions, which is dedicated to creating and delivering the professional services that help people clarify goals, improve relationships, and make smooth life and work transitions. Through her programs, she seeks to maximize the potential of individuals, teams, and organizations through intervention programs including: retention, performance improvement, change and transition issues, conflict resolution, communications, team development, executive and management coaching, outplacement, career development, and strategic planning. Prior to her work as a consultant, Carole held a variety of management and training/organizational development positions in the financial services field. She was responsible for development of a sales curriculum that turned a bank training department into a profit center and earned the bank $300,000 in revenue.

David Ellison, Napa, CA

David is an outstanding marketing and sales strategist, with a forte in plan/program execution and implementation. He has developed and marketed professional services products, thereby helping his clients to deal more effectively with business opportunities, profits, markets, and change. David's project management skills focus on strategic, tactical, and operational/marketing issues as they concern growth and profitability. He has worked extensively in consumer products, professional service, high-tech, and distribution industries worldwide.

William Meyer, Menlo Park, CA

William has expert knowledge of call center measurements, processes, and techniques—for example, load leveling software to improve call center service. For Seagate Technology, as Director of Telecom, he pioneered a conversion at Seagate's Technical Support to an Aspect ACD that improved service and reduced expense. He has gained excellent experience from time with AT&T, Transamerica, PG&E, and Seagate Technologies. Consulting assignments include: Inmac, VLSI Technology, The California Pacific Medical Center, Kaiser Permanente, Silicon Valley Bank, London Electricity (assignment in England), and Webcor Builders. His assignments focus on RFP preparation, project management, call center results and productivity improvement, voice processing systems, telecommunications systems, networks management, etc.

Jolanda de Boer, Oakland, CA

Jolanda de Boer is a hands-on manager with eight years of classic brand management and marketing consulting experience for Fortune 500 leaders such as Clorox, The Gap, The Coca-Cola Company, and Oral-B. Her experience covers developing and managing brands in all phases of the product life cycle, including new product development, in highly competitive markets. As a brand manager for The Coca-Cola Company, she developed and executed a highly effective strategy for their No.2 soft drink, which resulted in an increase of consumer awareness by 50%. Her responsibilities have included strategic planning, brand positioning, market research, packaging, promotions, POS, advertising, direct marketing, and budget management.

Paul Thode, Oakland, CA

Paul has direct experience working with customer accounting and charge back deductions, the bulk of which was in the apparel business. A strong accounting background and an M.B.A. back his extensive experience. He is very good at building and reorganizing accounting and operations areas, and where needed, creating new systems, training the staff upon implementation, and delegating the operational responsibility in a timely and effective manner.

Hazel Payne, Berkeley, CA

Hazel is a compensation consultant with a wide variety of experiences across industries. She has had experience with CSAA, Blue Shield, and Kaiser in developing, implementing, and administering compensation programs. She recently completed a complex, quantitative compensation project for Microsoft. She is a very detail-oriented team player and problem solver.

Dale Uptegrove, Berkeley, CA

Dale is a seasoned financial consultant with broad-based experience in mergers and acquisitions. He has worked extensively on large, capital-intensive projects, including acting as Acquisition Manager for Chevron's overseas petroleum business, planning and implementing all acquisitions in the international arena. He recently completed the formation of two internal equipment leasing companies for Kaiser Permanente that are expected to have a capitalization of about $500 million. Dale is comfortable in both large cor-porate environments and small entrepreneurial companies.

Dan Kleinman, San Francisco, CA

Dan is a guru in the area of developing and integrating base and variable pay programs, benefits structures, and non-tra-ditional reward systems that reinforce a company's direction and message. He has a rich background in compensation and benefits as a consultant and as a line officer in some large organizations, including Charles Schwab. He has developed total cash compensation plans and structures across various industries, corporate cultures, and business priorities. He has worked with Boards, CEOs, HR managers, and various staff specialists to develop near-term and longer-range programs that impact all employee groups—executive to first-line staff—and board members as well. His clients include M².

Jim White, Walnut Creek, CA

Jim has in-depth experience in consulting with his own company for nearly a decade. His clients have included PG&E, Southern California Edison, National Semiconductor, and Oracle as well as small wineries in northern California. Prior to going out on his own, he managed a wide range of information technology areas for the Du Pont company and Charles Schwab. His experience includes five years living and working in Europe. He maintains current contacts in the information technology industry throughout the world. He also has earned a C.M.C. and C.D.P.

Margery Mayer, San Carlos, CA

Margery Mayer specializes in strategy development, espe-cially in the IT arena, where she provides systems devel-opment, software development, and resourcing and systems integration. Margery has developed, in conjunction with the clients' life cycle methodologies, deliverables that were critical to developing corporate, worldwide IT solutions. Margery has been asked by her ongoing clients to manage multiple vendors contracted to deliver critical software engines and reports. Recently, Margery developed a strategy for sourcing IT projects for the next generation of systems of a major financial corporation, where she identified current staff skills and trends in project staffing, reskilling methodologies, and finally, strategies for sourcing from diverse suppliers of resources.

Sheila Wilkins, Walnut Creek, CA

Sheila has several years' experience within financial institutions and high-tech and manufacturing corporations. Her Certificate in Human Resources Management complements her extensive experience managing HR functions in both banking and high-technology organizations. She has facilitated an HR organization through two major restructuring efforts resulting in an overall consistent, customer-focused strategy throughout the bank. She also has organizational development savvy, which includes designing and implementing a performance improvement strategy for an Asian-owned and -managed bank. She trained over 800 people of different cultures on the bank's new computer system and new products and services. The results were overall buy-in and support of performance improvement strategies.

Whitney Vosburgh, Berkeley, CA

Whitney is a professional marketing consultant with extensive experience in lead/revenue generation, direct marketing, sales promotion, technology marketing, brand development, and team building. He is a former interim VP of Marketing at Quote.com and has more than ten years of experience at corporations, start-ups, and marketing agencies with management and P&L responsibility. His client experience includes IBM, Lotus, Compaq, Apple, and Advance Technology Staffing. He has strong interpersonal, leadership, communication, management, and creative skills.

Stephen Austin, Mill Valley, CA

Stephen has over 20 years of significant line and staff experience in key marketing and finance positions, primarily with entrepreneurial organizations, requiring a great deal of initiative and ability to act independently. He bought and sold leveraged and single-investor leases, and arranged debt for a major equipment leasing syndicator, which accounted for over 80 percent of the business booked by company. He managed five regional offices with 25 people for all U.S. marketing and operations for an international transportation company. A successful consultant for years, his clients include blue chip firms like Levi Strauss as well as not-for-profit organizations.

INDEX

Power Partnering: A Strategy for Business Excellence in the 21st Century,
Sean Gadman, 0-7506-9809-8

Putting Emotional Intelligence to Work: Successful Leadership Is More Than IQ,
David Ryback, 0-7506-9956-6

Resources for the Knowledge-Based Economy Series

The Knowledge Economy,
Dale Neef, 0-7506-9936-1

Knowledge Management and Organizational Design,
Paul S. Myers, 0-7506-9749-0

Knowledge Management Tools,
Rudy L. Ruggles, III, 0-7506-9849-7

Knowledge in Organizations,
Laurence Prusak, 0-7506-9718-0

The Strategic Management of Intellectual Capital,
David A. Klein, 0-7506-9850-0

Knowledge, Groupware and the Internet,
David Smith, 0-7506-7111-4

Knowledge and Communities,
Eric L. Lesser, Michael A. Fontaine, and Jason A. Slusher, 0-7506-7293-5

Knowledge and Social Capital,
Eric L. Lesser, 0-7506-7222-6

Strategic Learning in a Knowledge Economy
Robert Cross and Sam Israelit, 0-7506-7223-4

COMEDY IS DYING

PAUL CONSTANT

FRED HARPER

LEE LOUGHRIDGE

ROB STEEN

AHOY COMICS

TARA WAS BESIDE ME FOR
THIS WHOLE DARK RIDE, AND
THAT'S WHY I WOULDN'T
CHANGE A SINGLE SECOND.

– PAUL CONSTANT

I'VE NEVER HAD THE OPPORTUNITY TO DEDICATE A BOOK.
I HAVE TO DEDICATE THIS FIRST ONE TO MY PARENTS,
FRED AND JACKIE HARPER, FOR WHATEVER IT WAS THEY
DID TO MAKE ME AN ARTIST. I BLAME THEM BOTH.

– FRED HARPER

COMICSAHOY.COM   🐦 @ AHOYCOMICMAGS

HART SEELY - PUBLISHER
TOM PEYER - EDITOR-IN-CHIEF
FRANK CAMMUSO - CHIEF CREATIVE OFFICER
STUART MOORE - OPS
SARAH LITT - EDITOR-AT-LARGE
CORY SEDLMEIER - COLLECTIONS EDITOR

DAVID HYDE - PUBLICITY
DERON BENNETT - PRODUCTION COORDINATOR
KIT CAOAGAS - MARKETING ASSOCIATE
HANNA BAHEDRY - PUBLICITY COORDINATOR
LILLIAN LASERSON - LEGAL
RUSSELL NATHERSON SR. - BUSINESS

SNELSON

COMEDY IS DYING

PAUL CONSTANT	WRITER
FRED HARPER	ARTIST
LEE LOUGHRIDGE	COLOR
ROB STEEN	LETTERS
FRED HARPER	COVERS & LOGO
JOHN J. HILL	DESIGN
DERON BENNETT	ASSOCIATE EDITOR
TOM PEYER	EDITOR
CORY SEDLMEIER	COLLECTION EDITOR

CREATED BY **PAUL CONSTANT** AND **FRED HARPER**

CONTENTS

SNELSON: COMEDY IS DYING

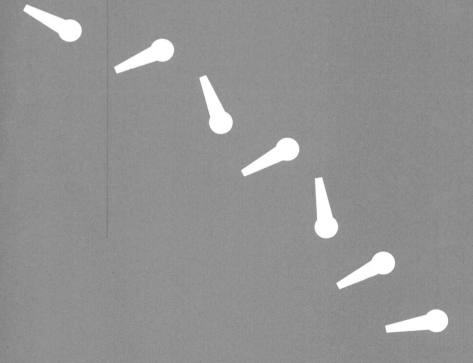

INTRODUCTION

In the beginning you could say whatever you want, joke about whomever you choose, use whatever words you please, and if it was funny, it was funny. Nothing else mattered. People laughed and were happy and all was good. The sun shone across the land.

Then one day the sun withdrew her favor and dark clouds fell. No longer was it safe to be a comedian. If you used a naughty word, the mob came for you. If you were accused of a naughty deed, the mob came for you. If you did a naughty deed, just one time, or even several times, the mob came for you. One by one the forces of illiberalism tore down every great comedian and even some lesser ones. When they were through, all that remained of a once-sacred art form was bland, toothless subservience to the gods of conformity.

Or, no, my mistake. What actually happened was a new golden age of comedy. These days you can get away with anything if you make the right people laugh. Hate speech, abuse, dalliances with neo-Nazis—they're all fodder for hundred-million-dollar deals, sold-out arenas, and fancy primetime awards. The mob is a pain in the ass, sure, but it's nothing compared to the *other* mob: the one rushing to fill your pockets just because the first one came after you. It's big business, being an asshole. So what are all these assholes complaining about?

Look no further than Melville Snelson for your answer. In the '90s he had it all: powerhouse agent, development deal, standup specials, hot festival gigs, the life most comedians dream of. Now he's touring the Deep South with a crew of younger comics who don't need him on the bill nearly as much as he needs them. One mishap leads to another, and before anyone can say "woke" he's ditching his set for a tirade against cancel culture. Haven't you heard? You can't say anything anymore. Enough is enough. If Snelson can't save comedy, he's ready to die with it—though somehow you get the feeling he'd prefer Option A.

Like many self-proclaimed saviors of comedy, what Snelson really wants to save is himself. The great injustice of his business—well, one of them—is that the refuge it promises misfits like him is far more metaphorical than material. Some go in broken and end up rich; most go in broken and just sort of putz around for a while, struggling to gain purchase. This isn't *failure* any more than losing the lottery is failure, but it's also not a sign of comedy's demise. Unfortunately, it's the business functioning as designed.

Can you blame Snelson for turning to lies, grift, and white male resentment? Yes, and you should, and then you should blame the system that gives some comedians nine-figure paychecks and others drink tickets, especially if the first group *also* traffics in lies, grift, and white male resentment. Comedy is full of Snelsons. Hell, it's *run* by Snelsons, as the final panels of his story make delightfully clear. His great failing—well, one of them—is inconveniently the only real prerequisite for success: an utterly irrational refusal to give up, no matter how rough the going gets.

Faith, in other words. Like many great characters before him, Snelson is driven by a belief in something far greater than himself. And like any tragic hero, he's too preoccupied with himself to recognize it. This dynamic comes to life rather masterfully in "What's the Deal With Wrist Injuries?", rendered in gory detail by Fred Harper's unnerving, visceral artwork, an effortless dance between nauseating claustrophobia and humbling scale. I will not sully the sequence with paraphrase. Suffice it to say that only when Snelson comes face-to-face with the true power of his art—a power too many comedians prefer not to think about—is he able to see himself from the outside in. Would that we were all so lucky.

Seth Simons
2022

Seth Simons writes Humorism, *a newsletter about labor, inequality, and extremism in comedy. Go to https:// humorism.xyz to subscribe.*

COMEDY IS DYING

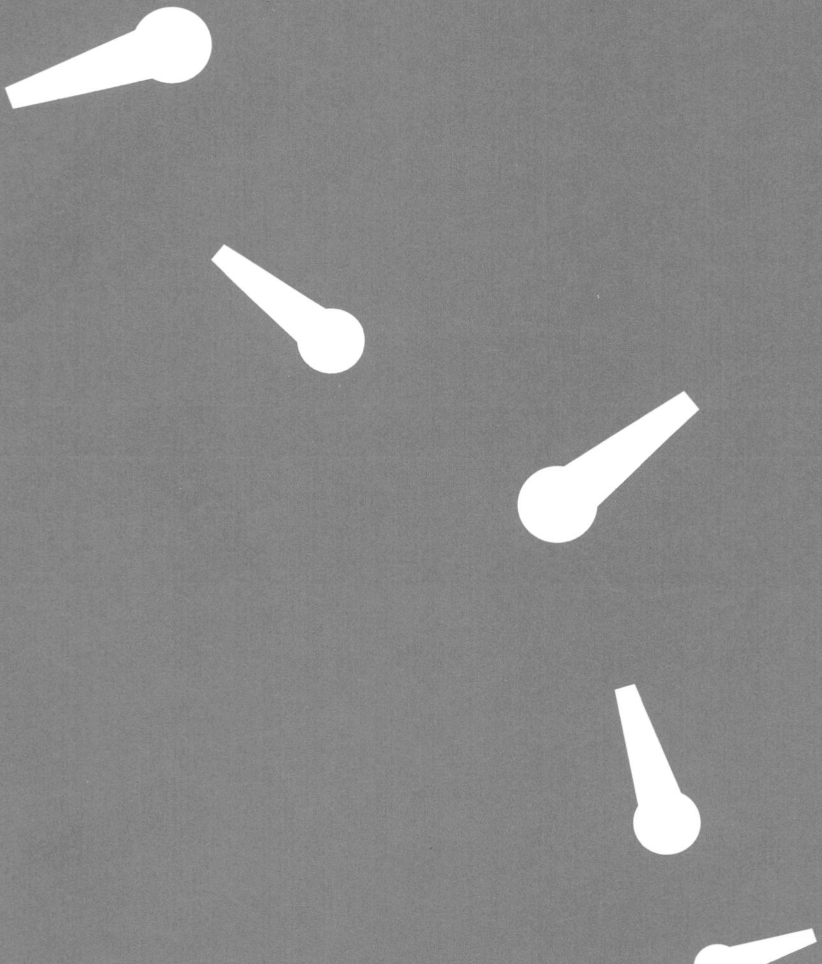

WHAT'S THE DEAL WITH WAITING IN LINE?

UH, *EXCUSE* ME...

AH, *CHRIST,* HERE WE GO.

YEAH?

AREN'T YOU... ARE YOU MELVILLE *SNELSON?*

THAT'S *ME.*

MY NAME'S DAVE. I WAS A BIG FAN OF YOURS. YOUR OPRAH'S BOOK CLUB BIT STILL CRACKS ME UP!

GREAT. THAT'S *GREAT* TO HEAR. THANKS.

I SAW YOU AT *LOLLAPALOOZA* IN '97, RIGHT? CORDUROY SUCCUBUS HEADLINED THAT YEAR!

YEAH, THAT WAS A *WILD* TOUR.

I *BET!*

SO ARE YOU STILL DOING *STAND-UP?*

I *HEADLINE* DOWN AT CHUCKLE'S GROTTO IN BROWNSVILLE EVERY THURSDAY.

FUCK, IS THIS LOSER FEELING *SORRY* FOR ME?

THAT'S JUST, LIKE, MY *HOME BASE*. I DROP BY THE COMEDY CELLAR EVERY ONCE IN A WHILE, TOO.

COOL, COOL.

HEY, WEREN'T YOU GOING TO DO A *SITCOM?* I READ THAT IN *TV GUIDE*, I THINK.

YEAH, BUT YOU KNOW THOSE HOLLYWOOD ASSHOLES, RIGHT? ALWAYS *COMPROMISING* AND *FOCUS-TESTING*...

THEY WANTED THE NEXT *JERRY SEINFELD* AND THAT'S NOT ME, YOU KNOW?

HA HA, NO KIDDING. YOU *SWEAR* A LOT MORE THAN HIM!

SO, UH, WHAT DO *YOU* DO, DAN?

DAVE, ACTUALLY. IT'S A FUNNY STORY.

I WAS BASICALLY A *POT DEALER* IN THE 90s.

I WORKED AT BORDERS BOOKS—REMEMBER THEM?— BUT I MADE *CASH* SELLING POT.

FUCK ME. THIS GUY IS SO *BORING*.

10

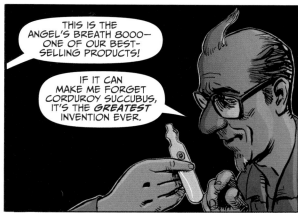

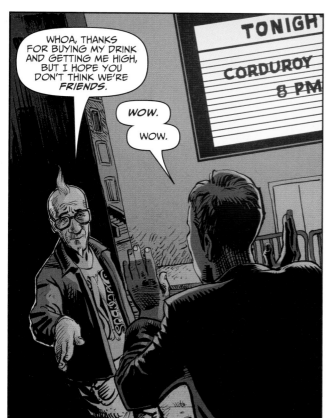

WHOA, THANKS FOR BUYING MY DRINK AND GETTING ME HIGH, BUT I HOPE YOU DON'T THINK WE'RE *FRIENDS*.

WOW.

WOW.

YOU KNOW, WHEN I WAS A KID I *IDOLIZED* YOU. YOU NEVER TOOK ANYONE'S BULLSHIT.

YOU'RE JUST A PROFESSIONAL *ASSHOLE*. I WAS GONNA ASK YOU TO PROMOTE THE ANGEL'S BREATH 8000, BUT NOW?

YOU CAN GO *FUCK* YOURSELF.

YOU THINK I EVEN *WANT* TO DO AN AD FOR YOUR SHITTY VAPE PEN?

I'M *NOBODY'S* CORPORATE WHORE!

13

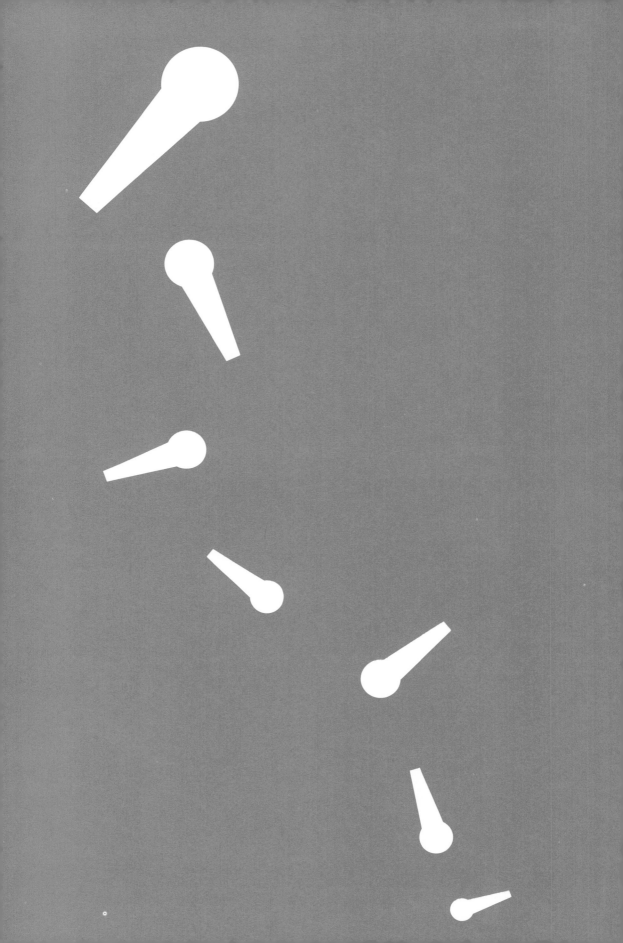

...AND THEN, *AFTER* I'VE WORN THE STUDIO EXECUTIVES DOWN WITH THE THREE UMBRELLAS STORY...

THAT'S WHEN I HIT 'EM WITH MY KILLER PITCH.

SEE, HARRISON FORD PLAYS A DISGRACED PRESIDENT. HE'S BEEN IMPEACHED AND ARRESTED.

AND SO THEY'RE SENDING HIM TO *PRISON*, ON A PLANE WITH THE WORST CRIMINALS IN THE COUNTRY.

SO THE OTHER CRIMINALS *HIJACK* THE FLIGHT AND HARRISON HAS TO STOP THEM AND PROVE HE'S BEEN FRAMED.

I CALL IT *CON AIR FORCE ONE TWO.*

WHAT'S THE DEAL WITH EATING IN RESTAURANTS?

THANK YOU! I AM MELVILLE SNELSON AND YOU HAVE BEEN A PERFECTLY *ADEQUATE* AUDIENCE.

CLAP

CLAP

CLAP

AND NOW GIVE A LOW-RENT CHUCKLE'S GROTTO WELCOME TO YOUR *FEATURED* PERFORMER, TABITHA TRAN!

THANK YOU! HERE'S A STORY THAT BEGINS IN *CHURCH* AND ENDS WITH ME GETTING PUNCHED IN THE CERVIX...

LATER...

HOLD ON A SEC.

IS YOUR RINGTONE A *NINE INCH NAILS* SONG?

IT'S A SPECIAL RING I SET FOR THIS ONE *EX* OF MINE.

YOU EXPECT ME TO BELIEVE YOU'VE EVER FUCKED *ANYONE*, MELVILLE?

FUNNY. SHE'S THE ONE I DUMPED FOR JANEANE. STILL *STALKS* ME SOMETIMES.

I'LL BE SURE 'DATED JANEANE GAROFALO' GOES ON YOUR *TOMBSTONE*. IT'S WHAT YOU WOULD'VE WANTED.

JESUS, COULD YOU SAY IT ANY *LOUDER?* I DON'T THINK THE DISHWASHER HEARD YOU IN BACK.

WELL, IT'S IMPORTANT THAT *EVERY* NEW RESTAURANT YOU VISIT KNOWS YOU WERE JANEANE'S BITCH.

REMIND ME *WHY* WE'RE FRIENDS, AGAIN?

16

BECAUSE I'M THE *ONLY* WOMAN IN COMEDY WHO CAN TOLERATE YOU.

RIGHT. LUCKY ME.

SO WHAT'S WITH THE NEW PLACE? DUNKIN' DONUTS ON QUEENS TOO *BASIC* FOR OUR POSTSHOW SNACK NOW?

I READ ABOUT IT ONLINE. IF YOU SLIP THE OWNER 20 BUCKS, HE COMES OUT AND *SINGS* TO YOUR TABLE...

YOU DIDN'T. TELL ME YOU *DIDN'T* DO THAT. YOU KNOW I HATE PUBLIC HUMILIATION.

I DIDN'T! I WAS HOPING HE'D SERENADE SOME *OTHER* TABLE. IT'S SUPPOSED TO BE HILARIOUS.

WHAT'D YOU THINK OF THE *CROWD* TONIGHT? PRETTY GOOD, RIGHT?

EHHH. KIND OF A *TOUGH* ROOM.

MY NEW STUFF ISN'T *WORKING* WITH THEM. I WONDER IF I SHOULD GO TRY THE CELLAR.

I MEAN, SURE. OR *MAYBE*... LOOK, MELVILLE. LISTEN...

17

THE HARRISON FORD JOKE IS TIGHT, BUT I DUNNO IF IT'S A *CLOSER*. THOSE MOVIES ARE PRETTY OLD...

AND THE '90S ARE BACK, RIGHT? IT'S A COMMENTARY ON REMAKE CULTURE.

AND THE THREE UMBRELLAS GAG... YOU KNOW, MOCKING EVANGELICALS ISN'T REALLY *KILLING* ANYMORE.

SO MY WHOLE ACT IS *SHITTY*? THAT'S WHAT YOU'RE SAYING?

NO, I'M JUST SAYING YOU SHOULD MAYBE INCORPORATE—THANK YOU—SOME *TIMELY* MATERIAL INTO THE ACT.

I'M NOT GOING TO DO A BUNCH OF "TRUMP IS BAD" GAGS. THEY'RE TOO *EASY*.

HEY, *SPEAKING* OF WHICH, HAVE YOU HEARD ABOUT GEOFF SARGENT?

UGH, DID HE FINALLY OVERDOSE?

NO, HE'S CLEAN. BUT HE'S DOING *ALT-RIGHT* COMEDY NOW.

WHAT DOES... I DON'T KNOW WHAT THAT MEANS.

18

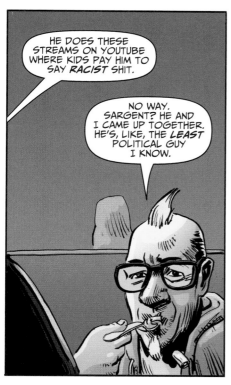

HE DOES THESE STREAMS ON YOUTUBE WHERE KIDS PAY HIM TO SAY *RACIST* SHIT.

NO WAY. SARGENT? HE AND I CAME UP TOGETHER. HE'S, LIKE, THE *LEAST* POLITICAL GUY I KNOW.

LOOK HIM UP. HE'S A TRUMP FAN. MAKING *MAD BANK,* TOO, AS THE KIDS SAY.

HUH.

IS HIS MATERIAL *GOOD?*

I MEAN, NO. WHAT? IT'S *DISGUSTING.* I ONLY WATCHED FIVE MINUTES OR SO.

SURE, BUT IT'S TIMELY, RIGHT? AND *TIMELY* IS GOOD. YOU JUST SAID.

OH, *GOD.* HERE WE GO.

I JUST WANT TO KNOW WHAT *KIND* OF TIMELY MATERIAL I NEED TO MAKE MY ACT BETTER.

FORGET I SAID ANYTHING, MELVILLE. OKAY?

21

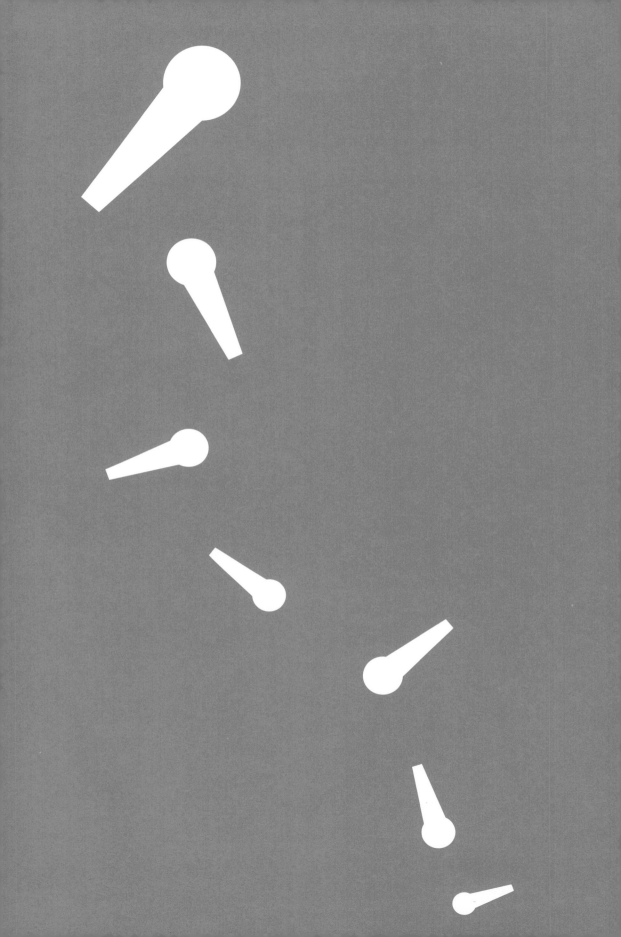

WHAT'S THE DEAL WITH AGENTS?

...I FELL ON SOME HARD TIMES. I MEAN, *REALLY* HARD TIMES. IT'S TOUGH FOR GUYS LIKE US TO MAKE A LIVING. *YOU* GET IT.

SURE.

SO I STARTED A YOUTUBE CHANNEL AND ATTRACTED THIS *AUDIENCE.* NOW I MAKE FIVE FIGURES A MONTH.

A *MONTH?* YOU'RE PULLING MY LEG.

SWEAR TO GOD. I JUST TELL A BUNCH OF AUTISTIC COMPUTER PROGRAMMERS WHAT THEY WANT TO HEAR AND THEY BACK A DUMP TRUCK OF *CASH* UP TO MY VENMO.

BUT WHAT YOU'RE SAYING-- YOU DON'T BELIEVE IT, RIGHT? ALL THAT CRAP ABOUT *SJWS* AND *NPCS?*

IT'S COMEDY. DO *YOU* BELIEVE EVERYTHING *YOU* SAY ONSTAGE?

BESIDES, I'M NOT AS HARDCORE AS OTHER GUYS. MOSTLY I TALK ABOUT *VIDEO GAMES* AND *COMIC BOOKS* AND SHIT.

WITH YOUR NEW LOOK, I'M SURPRISED YOU'RE NOT RUNNING A *BEAUTY SECRETS* CHANNEL.

FUCK YOU, MAN. *YOU* ASK *ME* TO MEET UP, YOU'RE TWENTY MINUTES LATE, AND THEN YOU MAKE FUN OF ME?

I'M JUST *JOKING*, LIKE WE USED TO! YOU LOOK *GREAT*, GEOFF. I WISH I COULD GET IN SHAPE LIKE YOU.

EH, IT'S JUST CALORIES IN, CALORIES OUT. TWO YEARS AGO, I WAS DEEP-THROATING DONUTS. NOW I'M SMASHING *PUSS*.

UH, COOL. SO WHAT MADE YOU DECIDE TO...AH, *SHIT*, HOLD ON, SORRY.

SORRY ABOUT THAT. THIS *EX* KEEPS CALLING ME.

HA! SAY NO *MORE*, MY MAN. IS THAT WHY YOU WERE LATE? FIGHTING 'EM OFF WITH A STICK?

Jeannie Ebbets mobile

NO, I'M LATE BECAUSE I WAS VISITING MY AGENT. *MARGE SUNDERSON*, KNOW HER?

LARGE MARGE? SHE'S *STILL* YOUR AGENT? ISN'T SHE, LIKE, A THOUSAND YEARS OLD?

UH, HERE'S THE THING...

"SHE WASN'T GIVING ME THE ATTENTION I DESERVED, SO I WAS READING HER THE RIOT ACT..."

HAVE YOU FOUND ANY GIGS, MARGE? THE GROTTO'S DRYING UP AND THAT WAS MY LAST STEADY THING.

SUNDERSON AGENCY

HAVE I "FOUND ANY GIGS?" YOU MEAN, LIKE THE LAST SIX GIGS THAT YOU BOTCHED?

ONE OF THOSE INVOLVED DRESSING UP LIKE A CLOWN. I DON'T DO COSTUME WORK.

"...MARGE HAS A REPUTATION FOR BEING MEAN, BUT I WAS REALLY HITTING HER HARD."

BACK WHEN EVERYONE WANTED YOU, YOU DIDN'T DO COSTUME WORK. NOW, YOU DO WHATEVER I FUCKING WELL GIVE YOU.

UH, I MEANT TO SAY I DON'T KNOW HOW TO DO COSTUME WORK. I JUST-- DAMMIT.

"...AND THAT WAS WHEN YOU CALLED TO SAY YOU WERE AVAILABLE TO MEET UP."

SORRY, I HAVE TO TAKE THIS.

YOU HAVE NO FOCUS, MELVILLE! THAT'S WHY YOU LOST THE SITCOM AND THAT'S WHY YOU LOSE EVERYTHING!

• • •

"...BUT WHEN I GOT OFF THE PHONE AND WALKED BACK INTO HER OFFICE, I FOUND..."

UH, MARGE? I HAVE TO GO MEET UP WITH GEOFF SARGENT. DO YOU REMEMBER HIM? HE-- MARGE?

"...SHE WAS *GONE*."

MARGE? ARE YOU OKAY? *MARGE?*

SHE *DIED?* HOLY SHIT! MARGE SUNDERSON DIED?

I CALLED THE PARAMEDICS, BUT IT WAS TOO *LATE*. AND THEN I RAN TO MEET YOU.

THIS IS AMAZING. I'M *JEALOUS* OF YOU, DUDE. THIS IS GOING TO MAKE AN AMAZING BIT.

I CAN'T DO A BIT ABOUT MARGE *DYING!* WHAT KIND OF MONSTER DO YOU THINK I AM?

WE'RE ALL MONSTERS IN THE COMEDY BUSINESS, BROTHER. IF THE TABLES WERE TURNED, MARGE WOULD'VE *LOOTED* YOUR CORPSE.

IT'S JUST SINKING IN. I DON'T HAVE AN *AGENT* ANYMORE.

I *FIRED* MY AGENT MONTHS AGO. YOUTUBE IS THE FUTURE OF COMEDY, MAN. I'LL HELP YOU GET STARTED.

I JUST DON'T KNOW IF I CAN PLAY TO THE *PROUD BOY* CROWD.

LOOK AT IT THIS WAY: IF I WASN'T DOING IT, IT WOULD BE SOMEBODY WAY *WORSE* THAN ME.

UH, EXCUSE ME?

WHY, *HELLO* THERE!

AREN'T YOU THAT GUY WHO CALLED MAZ FROM *STAR WARS* A *"PRETENTIOUS FUCKHOLE"* AND THREATENED TO *RAPE* HER?

MAYBE YOU DIDN'T GET THE MEMO-- STAR WARS CHARACTERS AREN'T *REAL.* QUIT BEING SO SENSITIVE, SNOWFLAKE.

I'M BEING SENSITIVE?

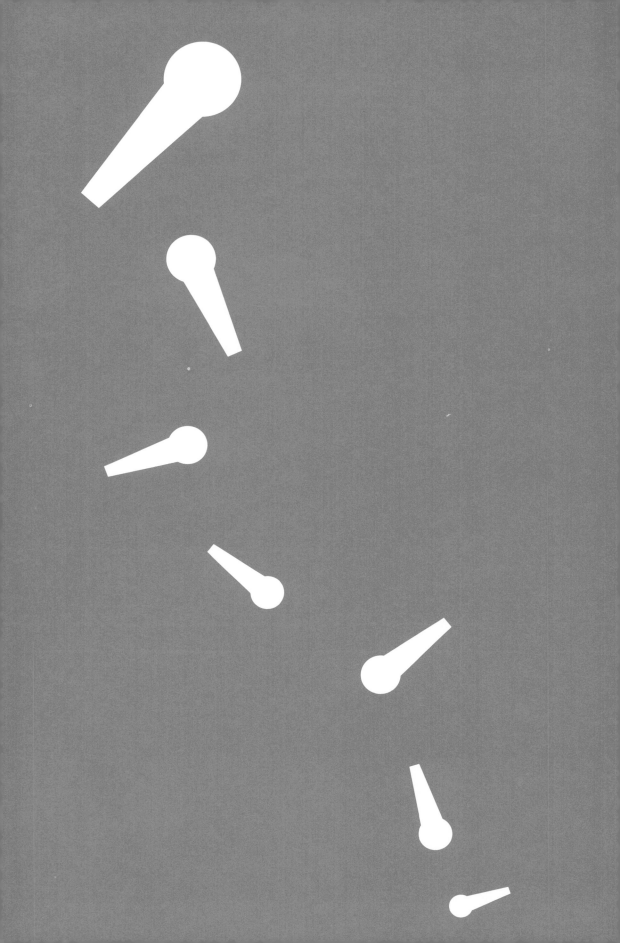

WHAT'S THE DEAL WITH MANHATTAN?

HELLO! *HI!* HELLO! LIKE THE MAN SAID, MY NAME IS MELVILLE SNELSON.

CLAP CLAP CLAP

THANK YOU. I'M *THRILLED* TO BE HERE TONIGHT.

CLAP CLAP

AN *HONOR* TO BE HERE IN MANHATTAN.

ACTUALLY, I'M LYING. IT'S *NEVER* AN HONOR TO BE IN MANHATTAN. ONLY TOURISTS AND DAY TRADERS LOVE MANHATTAN.

LAST TIME I WAS IN MANHATTAN, I SAW SOMETHING *WEIRD*.

I'M UP HERE, I MIGHT AS WELL TELL YOU ABOUT IT.

I HAD AN APPOINTMENT. YOU DON'T CARE WHY. IT WAS AROUND 5 O'CLOCK, SO *RUSH HOUR* WAS UNDERWAY.

SOME *TECH* START-UP HAD JUST LET OFF WORK. THE KIND OF THING WHERE YOU SELL YOUR MOM'S VITAL ORGANS THROUGH AN APP.

MEANWHILE, JUST A FEW FEET AWAY, A HOMELESS GUY IS HAVING A *PSYCHOTIC BREAK* ON THE SIDEWALK.

I MEAN, HE WAS SAYING *CRAZY* SHIT.

"DONALD TRUMP *DID NOTHING WRONG*" KIND OF CRAZY SHIT. IMPLAUSIBLE STUFF.

BUT THEN, OUT OF NOWHERE...

WRONG!

THE HOMELESS GUY JUST PICKED THIS **ONE GUY** OUT OF THE CROWD, TOTALLY AT RANDOM.

HE'S STILL **SHOUTING** SHIT LIKE

"MERYL STREEP IS WILDLY **OVERRATED** AS AN ACTRESS!"

YOU KNOW, THINGS NO SANE PERSON WOULD **EVER** SAY IN PUBLIC.

AND THE HOMELESS GUY JUST FUCKING HAULS OFF AND **SMACKS** THIS RANDOM GUY. LIKE MIKE FUCKING TYSON!

BUT **THAT** WASN'T THE WEIRD PART. THE WEIRD PART CAME NEXT.

VERY SLOWLY, THE GUY WHO GOT HIT BENT *DOWN*...

...*PICKED* UP HIS GLASSES...

...AND PUT THEM BACK *ON*.

AND THEN EVERYBODY JUST KEPT GOING LIKE NOTHING HAPPENED. THE CRISIS HAD BEEN *AVERTED*.

BUT I REALIZED THAT WESTERN CIVILIZATION IS ALWAYS, LIKE, ONE BAD CUSTOMER SERVICE INTERACTION AWAY FROM *COLLAPSING* ENTIRELY.

HA HA

MY AGENT *DIED* A COUPLE MONTHS AGO. I WAS IN THE OFFICE WHEN SHE STROKED OUT.

THE TRUTH IS, SHE *HATED* ME AND I *HATED* HER.

SHE WAS TELLING ME HOW *WORTHLESS* I WAS WHEN SHE DIED. LIKE, SHE WAS MID-SENTENCE AND THEN—BAM!

AT LEAST SHE DIED DOING WHAT SHE *LOVED*, I GUESS. BUT IT REMINDED ME—

YOU GOING TO BE *FUNNY?*

UH, *WOW.* EXCUSE ME?

ARE YOU GOING TO TELL *JOKES,* OR ARE YOU JUST GOING TO WHINE ABOUT YOUR LIFE?

I THOUGHT THIS WAS WHAT EVERYONE *WANTED* NOW. "NANETTE," RIGHT? EVERYONE LOVES HANNAH GADSBY WHEN SHE...

YEAH, *YOU'RE* NO HANNAH GADSBY.

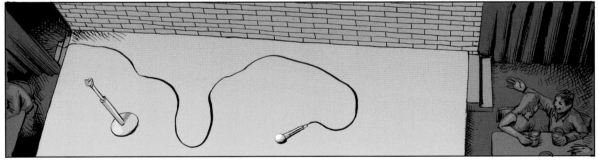

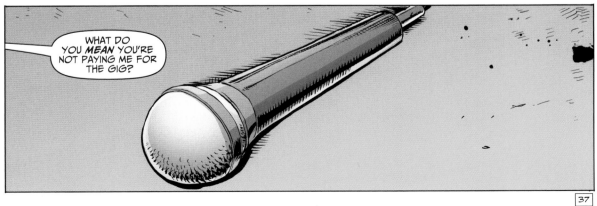

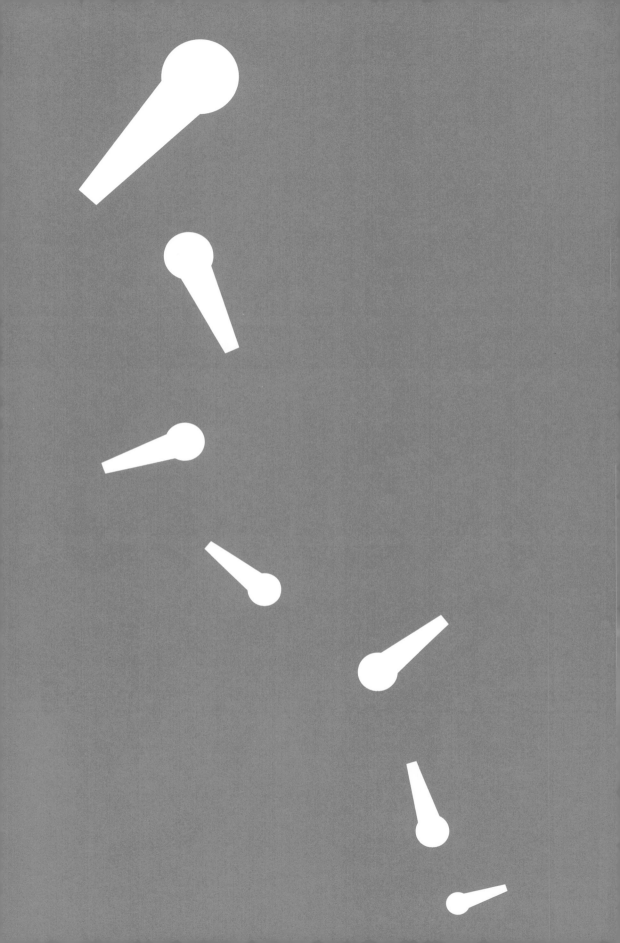

WHAT'S THE DEAL WITH THE INTERNET?

HAILCAESAR SAYS:
is it tru eyou dated Jeanine Garrufalo? ($1)

HAILCAESAR SAYS:
sorry sorr yforgot

HAILCAESAR:
right

TRUNPPEMCE: 😄 I Made Two Dollars An Hour Shoveling Horse Shit In The 70s And It Sucked LOLOL

RIGHT, SO HAILCAESAR HAS A *SUPERBOX* QUESTION ABOUT WHETHER I DATED JANEANE. HONESTLY, A GENTLEMAN SHOULD NEVER KISS AND TELL.

SO I GUESS I'M NOT TELLING YOU ANYTHING A FEW *THOUSAND* TIMES OVER, IF YOU KNOW WHAT I MEAN. THANKS, HAILCAESAR!

WHOA, WE'VE GOT ANOTHER SUPERBOX QUESTION FROM A *NEW USER*, GUYS! LET'S SEE...

DAPPERWHITEY SAYS:
SAY "HITLER DID NOTHING WRONG" ($5)

JUMBOTRON SAYS:
i saw you at lolapalooza u were 😄

TRUNPPEMCE SAYS:
Who Is Jeane Anne?

HAILCAESAR SAYS:
wow lucky dog!

41

UH, DAPPERWHITEY, WELCOME. BUT THAT'S NOT REALLY WHAT THE SUPERBOX IS *FOR*. IF YOU HAVE ANY QUESTIONS...

DAPPERWHITEY SAYS: WILL YOU SAY "HITLER DID NOTHING WRONG" FOR FIFTY DOLLARS? ($50)

JUMBOTRON: lol your bit about urkel still has me 😂😂😂

TRUNPPEMCE: I Always Enjoy Your Streamtoobs.

DAPPERWHITEY SAYS: SAY "HITLER DID NOTHING WRONG" ($5)

SO DAPPERWHITEY WANTS ME TO SAY, UH... HE WANTS ME TO *SAY* THE PHRASE *"HITLER DID NOTHING WRONG."*

THANKS, DAPPERWHITEY. OH, GUYS, GUESS WHAT? IT'S FINALLY NEW *BILLBOARD* DAY!

THERE ARE LIKE *FIFTY* NEW PEOPLE ON THE STREAM TODAY, SO YOU MIGHT NOT KNOW THE SAGA OF THE BILLBOARD.

SO THE BILLBOARD ACROSS THE STREET FROM MY PLACE HAS HAD THE SAME SAD-ASS *BURGER KING* AD FOR THREE YEARS.

BUT YESTERDAY, THEY STARTED PUTTING A *NEW* AD UP! I HAVEN'T PEEKED, SO YOU CAN WITNESS MY REACTION AS I SEE IT FOR THE FIRST TIME.

HERE GOES...

THE NEW Angel's Breath 9000

"It's the BEST thing I've put in my mouth all month!" (sorry Doug 😊)

Tabitha Tran
Comedian

GUYS, YOU EVER HAVE A FRIEND *SCREW* YOU OVER?

OR HAS SOMEONE WHO WAS UNQUALIFIED EVER *STOLEN* SOMETHING OUT FROM UNDER YOU?

IT'S NOT *OKAY* ANYMORE TO ACCUSE SOMEONE OF BEING A DIVERSITY HIRE, BUT IF TALENT WAS ALL THAT MATTERED, THERE'S *NO* WAY—

KNOCK KNOCK

HOLD ON A MINUTE, GUYS. THIS MIGHT BE MY *HIGHER-QUALITY* WEBCAM. MAYBE WE'LL DO AN UNBOXING VIDEO.

HELLO?

MR. SNELSON? *HI.* MY NAME IS DANICA BAKSHI. I'M A REPORTER AT THE TEEN ECONOMIST.

THERE'S A *TEEN* VERSION OF THE ECONOMIST NOW?

HONESTLY, I THINK THEY JUST WANTED TO GET AWAY WITH PAYING THEIR WRITERS *LESS.*

LISTEN, I'M NOT INTERESTED IN A *HIT PIECE* ON ALT-RIGHT COMEDIANS OR WHATEVER IT IS YOU'RE DOING...

MR. SNELSON, I WANTED TO TALK TO YOU ABOUT *JEANNIE EBBETS*.

WHAT... WHAT *ABOUT* HER?

MR. SNELSON, JEANNIE SAYS YOU WERE IN A ROMANTIC RELATIONSHIP IN THE LATE 1990s, WHEN SHE WAS 15 AND YOU WERE IN YOUR *MID-20s*.

KA-CHUD

DO YOU HAVE ANY *COMMENT* FOR MY *READERS*, SIR?

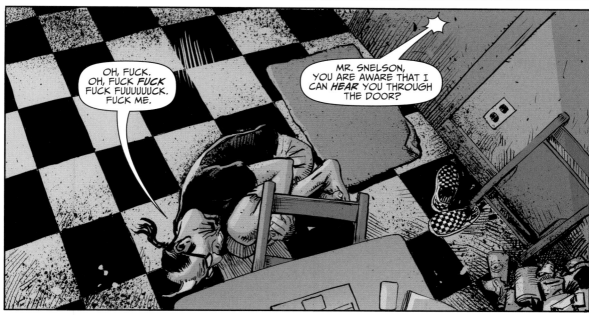

OH, FUCK. OH, FUCK *FUCK* FUCK FUUUUUUCK. FUCK ME.

MR. SNELSON, YOU ARE AWARE THAT I CAN *HEAR* YOU THROUGH THE DOOR?

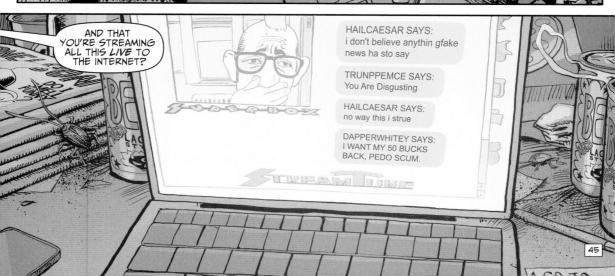

AND THAT YOU'RE STREAMING ALL THIS *LIVE* TO THE INTERNET?

HAILCAESAR SAYS:
i don't believe anythin gfake news ha sto say

TRUNPPEMCE SAYS:
You Are Disgusting

HAILCAESAR SAYS:
no way this i strue

DAPPERWHITEY SAYS:
I WANT MY 50 BUCKS BACK, PEDO SCUM.

45

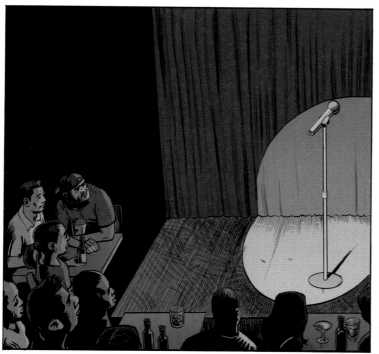

CLAP CLAP CLAP

THANK YOU, RALEIGH! MY NAME IS MELVILLE SNELSON. YOU MIGHT HAVE READ ABOUT ME BEING CANCELED LAST YEAR.

I DON'T HAVE A TV SHOW OR ANYTHING. I MEAN *I* WAS CANCELED. A REPORTER FOUND OUT I DATED A 17-YEAR-OLD WHEN I WAS 25 AND THEN--

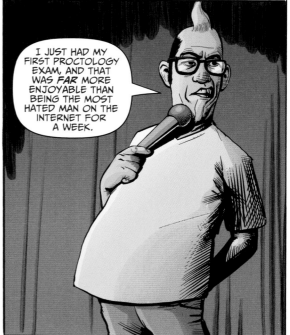

I JUST HAD MY FIRST PROCTOLOGY EXAM, AND THAT WAS *FAR* MORE ENJOYABLE THAN BEING THE MOST HATED MAN ON THE INTERNET FOR A WEEK.

SO LIKE EVERY OTHER COMEDIAN, I LIVE IN *BROOKLYN.* AND BROOKLYN HAS A BASKETBALL TEAM...

WOOO! GO NETS!

OKAY, *THAT* GUY'S CUT OFF. NO, SERIOUSLY, THANK YOU, SIR. IT IS THE NETS. NOW, PLEASE NEVER SPEAK AGAIN.

ANYWAY, ONE NIGHT I WAS HEADING HOME AT AROUND THE TIME THE NETS GAME WAS LETTING OUT.

WHO DECIDED THAT *"SHITTY TOILET PAPER* STUCK TO THE BOTTOM OF YOUR SHOE" WAS THE IDEAL WAY TO ADVERTISE ONLINE, ANYWAY?

SO ANYWAY, HERE'S MY IDEA: RATHER THAN SWITCH TO INCOGNITO MODE, GOOGLE SHOULD MAKE IT SO THAT WHENEVER YOU GOOGLE THE WORDS *"THE FUCK,"* THAT SEARCH DOESN'T SHOW UP IN YOUR SEARCH HISTORY.

SO, LIKE, *"IS THE FUCKING NETS GAME OVER?"*

YOU COULD DO THIS WITH ANYTHING YOU DON'T WANT GOOGLE TO REMEMBER ABOUT YOU.

"WHY THE FUCK ARE HIGH-WAISTED PANTS BACK IN STYLE?"

I WANTED TO KNOW IF I SHOULD STAY OUT AND HAVE ANOTHER DRINK TO *AVOID* GETTING STUCK IN TRAFFIC.

SO I WANTED TO GOOGLE TO FIND OUT IF I HAD TIME TO GET HOME. BUT THE THING IS, I *HATE* SPORTS.

AND I KNOW THAT IF I GOOGLED THE GAME, I'D HAVE *BASKETBALL ADS* TRAILING BEHIND ME EVERYWHERE ON THE INTERNET FOR TWO MONTHS.

"WHY THE FUCK IS *HULK HOGAN* TRENDING ON TWITTER?"

YOU KNOW, "WHAT THE FUCK IS THIS *FLOSS DANCE* BULLSHIT?"

"WHY THE FUCK DOES MY PROCTOLOGIST'S FINGER UP MY ASS MAKE ME THINK OF *GWYNETH PALTROW?*"

THANK YOU, NORTH CAROLINA! THANKS FOR JOINING AVIGAIL, CALVIN, DONNA AND I FOR THE *"GET WOKE OR DIE BROKE"* TOUR. GOOD NIGHT!

THE NEXT DAY...

RALEIGH MOTOR INN

HOW LONG TO *KNOXVILLE*, AGAIN?

SHOULD GET THERE AROUND SIX. WHAT DID EVERYONE THINK OF THE *SHOW* LAST NIGHT?

EH, I'VE HAD *WORSE*.

YOU'RE BEING MODEST, AVIGAIL. YOU *KILLED!* I STILL CAN'T GET MY *"OLD TOWN ROAD"* BIT TO LAND.

THE IMPORTANT THING IS THAT SNELSON DIDN'T GET ANY OF US *SHOT*.

A VEGAN JEW, A GIANT BLACK DUDE, AND A TRANS WOMAN TOURING THE DEEP SOUTH IN A RENTAL PRIUS, AND THE *MIDDLE-AGED WHITE GUY* IS GONNA CAUSE PROBLEMS?

YOU HAVE A *UNIQUE* ABILITY TO PISS PEOPLE OFF, SNELSON.

AT LEAST I'M *HONEST* ABOUT IT.

HONESTY IS *OVERRATED*, HONESTLY.

WE'RE DRAWING PRETTY *DECENT* CROWDS, THOUGH.

IT'S BEEN GOOD! I THINK WE'RE AN *APPEALING* MIX OF PEOPLE AND STYLES.

HOW ABOUT *YOU*, DONNA? WHAT'S BEEN WORKING FOR YOU?

I'M JUST GLAD SNELSON'S AGREED TO STOP REFERRING TO US AS HIS *"HUMAN SHIELDS."*

IT WAS A *JOKE!* IT'S COMEDY!

IS IT? I KINDA DOUBT YOU'D GET BOOKED *ANYWHERE* WITHOUT A POSSE OF SOCIAL JUSTICE WARRIORS ON THE BILL.

SERIOUSLY, HOW CAN ANYONE THINK THEY'RE *HAPPY* OUT THERE?

AGAIN WITH THE COWS?

STUDIES SHOW COWS HAVE COMPLEX *EMOTIONAL* LIVES.

WELL, I THINK WE'RE HITTING OUR *STRIDE.* THE NEXT THREE WEEKS ARE GOING TO JUST FLY BY--

SNELSON, LOOK OUT!

SKREEE

MUUUUR?

YOU'RE RIGHT, AVIGAIL. THE GRATITUDE I SEE IN THOSE *BIG BROWN EYES* FOR SPARING HER LIFE IS ALMOST HUMAN.

EAT SHIT, MELVILLE.

"WHY THE FUCK DOES MY PROCTOLOGIST'S FINGER UP MY ASS MAKE ME THINK OF GWYNETH PALTROW?"

THANK YOU, KNOXVILLE! GOOD NIGHT!

CAN I GET A *SEVEN AND SEVEN?* I'VE GOT A DRINK TICKET AROUND HERE SOMEWHERE...

I'LL BUY THAT SEVEN AND SEVEN, HENRY.

YOU REALLY DON'T *HAVE* TO. THEY GIVE US FREE DRINKS.

BUT I *WANT* TO.

WELL, GIVEN THAT I CAN'T *FIND* MY SWEATY LITTLE DRINK TICKET RIGHT NOW, I'LL TAKE YOU UP ON THAT...

TINA.

TINA. SO, TINA...

SEE, I WAS *ABOUT* TO SAY "WHAT DID YOU THINK OF THE SHOW?" BUT I DON'T KNOW IF I WANT TO KNOW THE ANSWER.

WHAT? WHY?

WELL, WHAT IF YOU *HATED* IT?

HA! GET A LOAD OF MISTER *INSECURE* OVER HERE!

IF I HATED YOUR SHOW, WOULD I BE BUYING YOUR *DRINK* RIGHT NOW? CHEERS, BY THE WAY.

CHEERS.

ALTHOUGH...

OH BOY, HERE WE GO...

I THINK YOU'RE UNFAIR TO POOR GWYNETH. SHE'S A *STRONG WOMAN!*

YIKES, OKAY. WELL, I THINK WE MIGHT *DISAGREE* ON A FEW IMPORTANT ISSUES, SO THANKS FOR THE DRINK AND...

RELAX, MELVILLE. I'M STILL GONNA FUCK THE SHIT OUT OF YOU TONIGHT.

I'M SORRY, *WHAT?*

YOU HEARD ME, COWBOY. MEET ME OUT IN THE *PARKING LOT* IN TEN. I'M IN THE BURNT ORANGE PT CRUISER.

SNELSON. CAN I HAVE A *WORD?*

A QUICK ONE, YEAH. I THINK I HAVE, UH, A *DATE.*

ON MY FIRST DAY OF *KINDERGARTEN,* AS HE WAS DROPPING ME OFF AT SCHOOL, MY DAD GAVE ME SOME ADVICE.

THE *ONLY* ADVICE HE EVER GAVE ME. HE LOOKED ME IN THE EYES, LIKE I'M DOING RIGHT NOW, AND HE SAID...

HE SAID, "DON'T STICK YOUR DICK IN CRAZY."

UH, *WOW*, DONNA.

AFTER SCHOOL, HE DIDN'T COME TO PICK ME UP. *NEVER* SAW HIM AGAIN. HE'D SAID WHAT HE HAD TO SAY.

THAT'S A TOUCHING STORY, BUT I HAVEN'T GOTTEN LAID SINCE A *BILLIONAIRE* WAS MAYOR OF NEW YORK, SO I'M GONNA IGNORE IT.

BAD

I FIGURED-- JUST HAD TO TRY. NOW I'M GONNA GO TAKE A SWIG OF THAT *TALL DRINK OF WATER* OVER THERE.

ARE YOU *SURE?* DONNA, WE'RE IN THE DEEP SOUTH, HERE.

TRUST ME.

56

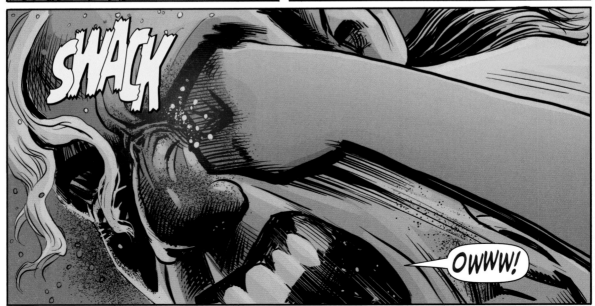

AND SO, THE NEXT NIGHT...

...AND YOU CAN KEEP YOUR DUMB JOKES ABOUT *MIKE PENCE* BEING A CLOSET CASE.

JESUS, WHY DON'T I EVER GET THESE NOTIFICATIONS WHEN THEY *HAPPEN?*

Today 11:38 AM
You have a new voicemail

WHAT DOES IT SAY THAT THE *BEST JOKE* YOU CAN MAKE ABOUT A RAGING HOMOPHOBE IS "HE PROBABLY LIKES TO SUCK DICK"?

MR. SNELSON, THIS IS DEBBIE FROM DR. LUNDEEN'S OFFICE. I'VE BEEN CALLING ALL WEEK AND THIS IS A MATTER OF SOME IMPORTANCE.

THERE'S AN *IRREGULARITY* WITH YOUR RECENT EXAM. WE'RE GOING TO NEED YOU TO COME IN FOR A *BIOPSY* AS SOON AS POSSIBLE.

THANK YOU FOR YOUR TIME. WE LOOK FORWARD TO HEARING FROM YOU.

...ALL THE WAY FROM, AS YOU NASHVILLE FOLKS CALL IT, "JEW YORK SHITTY," GIVE *A BIG HAND* FOR MELVILLE SNELSON!

I SAID, GIVE *A BIG HAND* FOR MELVILLE SNELSON, WHO WAS RECENTLY CONCUSSED IN A KNOXVILLE PARKING LOT!

AH!

DID YOU CATCH *EAR HERPES* FROM BOOBS RADLEY LAST NIGHT?

SORRY! SORRY!

UH, SO.

Donna Ritigio FAN CLUB

Laflflers

EXIT

UH, NASHVILLE...

SO, NASHVILLE. I KNOW I'M NOT SUPPOSED TO SAY THIS IN A COMEDY CLUB, BUT *COMEDY SUCKS NOW.*

I'VE BEEN DOING THIS FOR A LIVING FOR *DECADES.* I ALMOST HAD A SITCOM.

THIS, UH, ISN'T HIS TIGHT FIFTEEN.

I HUNG OUT WITH, LIKE, JANEANE GAROFALO. BACK WHEN THAT *MATTERED.* BUT NOW? NOTHING'S FUNNY ANYMORE.

KNOW WHY NOTHING'S FUNNY ANYMORE? BECAUSE *EVERYBODY THINKS THEY'RE FUNNY* NOW.

GIVE ANY ASSHOLE A TWITTER LOGIN AND HE THINKS HE'S *LENNY FUCKING BRUCE.* FUCK THAT.

OH, NO! HE'S WHINING ABOUT THE *GOOD OLD DAYS!*

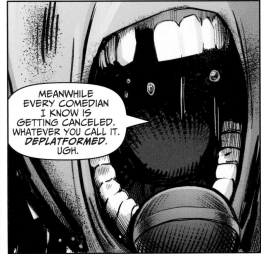

MEANWHILE EVERY COMEDIAN I KNOW IS GETTING CANCELED. WHATEVER YOU CALL IT. *DEPLATFORMED.* UGH.

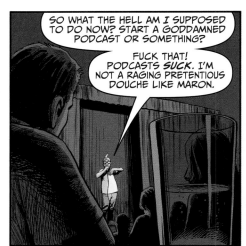

SO WHAT THE HELL AM *I* SUPPOSED TO DO NOW? START A GODDAMNED PODCAST OR SOMETHING?

FUCK THAT! PODCASTS *SUCK.* I'M NOT A RAGING PRETENTIOUS DOUCHE LIKE MARON.

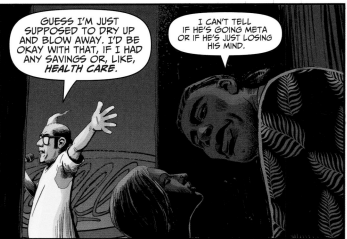

GUESS I'M JUST SUPPOSED TO DRY UP AND BLOW AWAY. I'D BE OKAY WITH THAT, IF I HAD ANY SAVINGS OR, LIKE, *HEALTH CARE.*

I CAN'T TELL IF HE'S GOING META OR IF HE'S JUST LOSING HIS MIND.

I DON'T HAVE A 401(K). I HAVE 11 HOURS OF MATERIAL I CAN'T *DO* ANYMORE BECAUSE IT'S NOT "POLITICALLY CORRECT," RIGHT?

HE KNOWS EXACTLY WHAT HE'S DOING.

I'M NOT AFRAID TO SAY IT, NASHVILLE: *COMEDY IS DYING.* AND I'M EITHER GOING TO SAVE IT, OR I'M GOING TO DIE WITH IT.

HE'S CRASHING HIS CAREER ON AN ICEBERG, AGAIN. AND HE'S TAKING *US* DOWN WITH HIM.

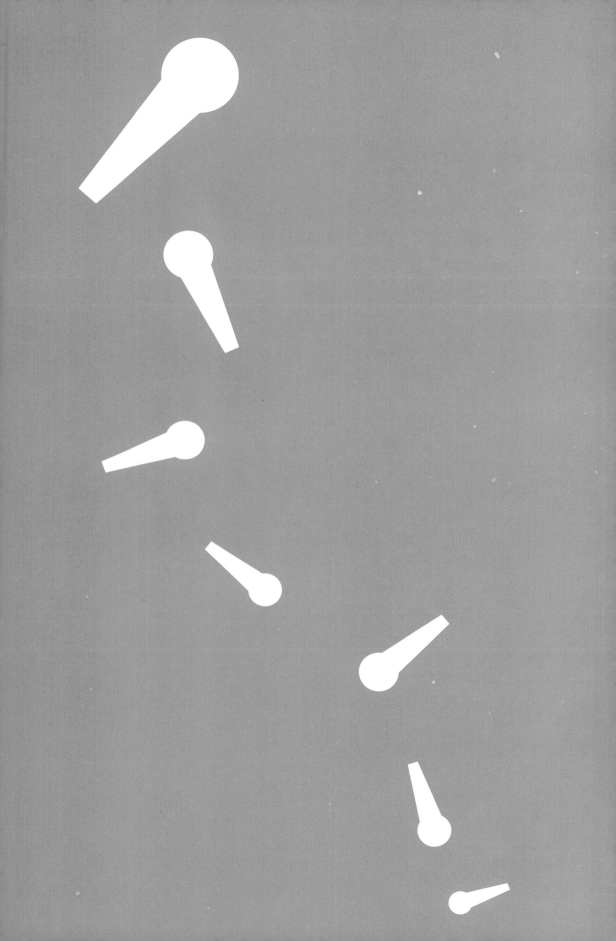

YOU MAY KNOW ME AS A DOCUMENTARIAN COVERING THE *WAR ON FREE SPEECH*, FROM CAMPUSES TO COMEDY CLUBS.

LYNZI IRWIN — PRODUCER, DIRECTOR, JOURNALIST

PERHAPS YOU'VE SEEN MY FILMS ON *YOUTUBE*: *THE CANCELING OF LOUIS CK*; *BARI WEISS: VICTIM, PROPHET-- OR BOTH?*; AND *THOUGHT CRIME U.*

"I'M A *TIRELESS* DEFENDER OF THE FREE MARKET OF IDEAS."

NO HATE SPEECH HARVARD

NO FASCISTS

FOOTAGE FROM *KKKAMPUS KKKONTROL: WHO ARE THE REAL NAZIS HERE?*

"I'M NOT AFRAID TO *RUFFLE SOME FEATHERS*."

LAKEWOOD'S SYLLABUS ERASES THE WORK OF IMPORTANT THINKERS LIKE JORDAN PETERSON AND JOE ROGAN!

LAKEWOOD COMMUNITY COLLEGE

FOOTAGE FROM *THOUGHT CRIME U*

"AND I SPEAK OUT ON BEHALF OF THOSE WHO HAVE HAD THEIR VOICES *SILENCED*."

SO SHAKESPEARE IN LOVE AND THE KING'S SPEECH NEVER *HAPPENED?* TINSELTOWN CAN'T SEPARATE ART FROM ARTIST?

FOOTAGE FROM *HARVEY WEINSTEIN: VICTIM OR MARTYR?*

I'M IN BROOKLYN TO TALK TO *A NEW VICTIM* OF THE INTERNET HATE MOB. HAS CANCEL CULTURE RUN AMOK? LET'S TALK ABOUT...

THE SILENCING OF MELVILLE SNELSON

HELLO AND WELCOME **BACK** TO *COMEDY IS DYING*, THE ONLY PODCAST THAT PULLS NO PUNCHLINES.

I'M YOUR HOST, MELVILLE SNELSON, AND WE'VE GOT A VERY *SPECIAL* SHOW FOR YOU TODAY.

IS COMEDY HEALTHY? IS IT DYING? MY GUEST HAS **LOTS** OF OPINIONS.

MELVILLE SNELSON — CANCELED STAND-UP COMEDIAN, PODCASTER

BILLY *CRYSTAL* ONCE CALLED HIM, AND I QUOTE, AN *"AMUSING YOUNG MAN."* NOW, HE'S COMPLETELY RADIOACTIVE.

I'M TALKING, OF COURSE, ABOUT **GEOFF SARGENT.**

'SUP, SNELSON?

GREAT TO HAVE YOU ON THE SHOW. LAST TIME I SAW YOU...

**GEOFF SARGENT —
FORMER COMEDIAN & ANTI-ANTIFA ACTIVIST**

"...SOME RANDO IN A PUSSY HAT **ASSAULTED** YOU! TALK ABOUT THAT."

"YEAH, I WAS MAKING PROVOCATIVE VIDEOS, AND MODERN AUDIENCES DON'T **GET** SATIRE ANYMORE. I KNOW THAT NOW."

FOOTAGE COURTESY TMZ

AFTER, WHEN WE WERE LOOKING FOR YOUR TOOTH, YOU SAID THAT HAPPENED TO YOU **ALL** THE TIME.

OH, YEAH. GOT PUNCHED LIKE SIX OR **EIGHT** TIMES.

DID YOU **DESERVE** IT?

I DON'T KNOW IF **ANYONE** DESERVES A KNUCKLE SANDWICH OVER A VIDEO ABOUT STAR WARS.

AND IT GOT **WORSE**, RIGHT?

YEAH. THREE PEOPLE THREW MILKSHAKES AT ME WHILE I WAS TAPING A SEGMENT. ONE WAS FROM **COLDSTONE CREAMERY**, FOR GOD'S SAKE!

TO BE FAIR: AT THE TIME, WEREN'T YOU WEARING A **SWASTIKA?**

71

I'VE NEVER EXPERIENCED ANYTHING WORSE THAN THE USPS, AND I WAS CIRCUMCISED AT 28!

TWO MEN, *SILENCED* BY THE WOKE HATE MOB, AT ONE TABLE. *HUMBLING.*

I've literally experienced

I'D RATHER PAY DWAYNE "THE ROCK" JOHNSON TO STAND ON MY *BALLSACK* FOR 15 MINUTES THAN GO...TO THE POST...

...OFFICE?

ALL THE HATE I GET ON TWITTER IS WORTH IT--

--BECAUSE I FIGHT FOR *THEIR* RIGHT TO SPEAK.

ONCE THEY SILENCE *SNELSON,* YOU CAN BE SURE THEY'RE COMING FOR YOU...

...NEXT?

HEY, UH, LYNZI? DO YOU MIND? WE'RE KINDA...RECORDING A *PODCAST* HERE...

"...YOU CAN TALK AFTER WE TAPE THE SHOW, OKAY?"

HOW DID YOU GET INVOLVED WITH THE PODCAST?

CALVIN TATU — PRODUCER, *COMEDY IS DYING* PODCAST

OKAY, SO, IN MY SPARE TIME I'M A COMIC. I WAS *TOURING* WITH SNELSON...

Snelson
AND ON THE LUNAR TIP

"...WHEN HE STARTED HIS 'COMEDY IS DYING' RIFF, AND THE CROWDS GOT *BIGGER* EVERY NIGHT!"

LISTEN, I GET THAT WOMEN SHOULDN'T BE SCARED TO BE BACKSTAGE AT COMEDY CLUBS, BUT LET'S BE *CLEAR* ABOUT SOMETHING...

HACK SHACK KOMEDY

FOOTAGE FROM *GET WOKE OR DIE BROKE* COURTESY MELVILLE SNELSON

"YOU COULD TELL SOMETHING *BIG* WAS HAPPENING. SNELSON WAS TAPPING INTO REAL EMOTIONS."

...COMEDY IS TRANSGRESSIVE, RIGHT? IF YOU'RE NOT FUCKING WITH SOMEONE'S *FEELINGS*, YOU'RE NOT BEING FUNNY!

YEAH!

YOU *TELL* 'EM, SWANSON!

FACTS DON'T CARE ABOUT YOUR FEELINGS!

75

SO I ASKED SNELSON IF HE EVER THOUGHT OF DOING A *PODCAST*, AND HERE WE ARE...

...NUMBER ONE ON APPLE'S ALT-COMEDY CHARTS, NUMBER SIX ON THEIR *ANTI-VAXX* CHARTS FOR SOME REASON...

ARE YOU PROUD TO WORK WITH AN ARTIST WHO HAS BEEN *SILENCED* BY THE HATE MOBS?

SORRY... DID YOU MISS WHEN I SAID WE'RE *POPULAR?* WE GET TENS OF THOUSANDS OF LISTENERS TWICE A WEEK...

FINALLY, IT'S TIME TO TALK TO THE *MAN* HIMSELF.

WE'VE GOT SO MANY ADVERTISERS THAT WE HAD TO TURN A MATTRESS COMPANY AWAY, AND *AZIZ ANSARI'S* COMING ON OUR NEXT EPISODE...

THANK YOU, CALVIN.

SO, MELVILLE...

PLEASE-- MELVILLE IS MY GREAT- GREAT-GREAT- *GRANDFATHER.* CALL ME SNELSON.

SO, SNELSON...

...WHAT PUSHED YOU TO THAT PLACE OF RADICAL *TRUTH- TELLING* WHEN YOU WERE ON TOUR?

UH, A REPORTER NAMED DANICA BAKSHI TALKED TO AN *EX* OF MINE WHO HAPPENED TO BE 17 WHEN WE DATED...

"...SHE WAS ABOVE THE AGE OF CONSENT, BUT EVERYONE CALLED ME A PEDOPHILE ANYWAY."

STEAMTOOB FOOTAGE COURTESY OF MELVILLE SNELSON

EPHEBOPHILIA.

...GESUNDHEIT?

NO, YOU SAID PEDOPHILIA, BUT ACTUALLY THAT'S JUST PEOPLE WHO PREY ON PREPUBESCENT KIDS. EPHEBOPHILIACS PREY ON TEENS.

JESUS, WHO CARES?

IT'S AN IMPORTANT DISTINCTION TO MAKE, BECAUSE...

MY POINT IS, I WAS 23 AT THE TIME AND I DON'T CARD MY LOVERS--

--SO I LOST IT ALL.

IS THERE ANYTHING YOU WANT ME TO ASK DANICA BAKSHI WHEN I INTERVIEW HER TOMORROW?

HOLD ON. WHAT?

THIS MOVIE'S SUPPOSED TO BE ABOUT ME.

I'M A JOURNALIST. OF COURSE I'M GOING TO INTERVIEW...

LOOK, I STRONGLY URGE YOU NOT TO TALK TO DANICA BAKSHI.

77

...AND ARE YOU STILL AT *TEEN ECONOMIST?*

NO, THEY FOLDED. NOW I WRITE FOR A PRESTIGE PUBLICATION FOUNDED BY A RENEWABLE *SNEAKER* BRAND.

DANICA BAKSHI
ALLBIRDS MONTHLY

SO I'M WORKING ON A DOCUMENTARY ABOUT THE *SILENCING* OF MELVILLE SNELSON AND I WANTED TO ASK YOU WHY--

HOW DO YOU FEEL ABOUT THE *ME TOO* MOVEMENT, LYNZI?

I'M NOT THE ONE BEING INTERVIEWED, HERE.

JEANNIE EBBETS JUST WANTED TO TALK TO MELVILLE. SHE WANTED CLOSURE. BUT HE *WOULDN'T* TALK TO HER.

SHE FELT *POWERLESS,* SO SHE CAME TO ME. I USED MY PLATFORM TO GIVE HER POWER.

SEE, JOURNALISTS DON'T COMFORT THE POWERFUL. WE AMPLIFY VOICES THAT *DESERVE* TO BE HEARD.

OKAY, IT'S CLEAR YOU'RE WORKING THROUGH SOME *ISSUES,* HERE...

I *KNOW* YOUR WORK. YOU'RE A CONSERVATIVE LAPDOG, AN APOLOGIST FOR PROUD BOYS AND 4CHAN CHUDS.

UH-HUH. A MARRIED *GAY* WOMAN IS THE NEXT TUCKER CARLSON. SURE.

I DON'T CARE IF YOU'RE CONSERVATIVE PERSONALLY OR NOT. YOU'RE DOING *THEIR* WORK FOR THEM.

YOU'RE A *USEFUL IDIOT.* REGRESSIVE DICKS HIDE BEHIND THEIR PET LESBIAN WHILE THEY BURN THE WORLD DOWN.

LET'S KEEP THIS ABOUT *SNELSON,* OKAY?

YOU DON'T GIVE A *SHIT* ABOUT MELVILLE. HE'S JUST CLICKBAIT. WHEN HE FUCKS UP, YOU'LL MOVE ON.

DO YOU EVER STOP MASTURBATING TO YOUR OWN BRILLIANCE AND ACTUALLY READ YOUR *COMMENTS,* LYNZI?

YOU'RE HOLDING *ME* RESPONSIBLE FOR MY COMMENTERS NOW?

NAZIS, BIGOTS, AND CREEPS *LOVE* YOU. EVER WONDER WHY? DID YOU EVER THINK FOR A SECOND ABOUT THAT?

OF COURSE YOU DIDN'T. BECAUSE YOU'RE *NOT* A FUCKING JOURNALIST OR A SOCIAL CRITIC. YOU'RE A CLOWN.

ALL *RIGHT!*

SMACK

FUCK YEAH!

COMBAT DYING

OKAY, I THINK SHE BOUGHT IT. LET'S SAY AZIZ IS *SICK.* I'VE ALREADY GOT A REPLACEMENT GUEST ON THE WAY.

GREAT THINKING! WHO IS IT?

AVIGAIL.

AVIGAIL SAPPERSTEIN? THE VEGAN *DWARF* FROM OUR TOUR? A BUCKET OF USED CONDOMS HAS MORE WARMTH THAN THAT VINDICTIVE LITTLE--

SHE'S MY *GIRLFRIEND,* SNELSON.

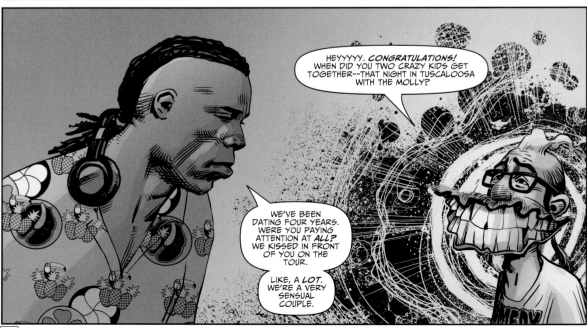

HEYYYYY. *CONGRATULATIONS!* WHEN DID YOU TWO CRAZY KIDS GET TOGETHER--THAT NIGHT IN TUSCALOOSA WITH THE MOLLY?

WE'VE BEEN DATING FOUR YEARS. WERE YOU PAYING ATTENTION AT *ALL?* WE KISSED IN FRONT OF YOU ON THE TOUR.

LIKE, A *LOT.* WE'RE A VERY SENSUAL COUPLE.

WELCOME BACK TO *COMEDY IS DYING*, THE ONLY PODCAST WILLING TO STAND UP AND TELL THE *TRUTH* ABOUT STAND-UP.

LOTS OF YOU HAVE REQUESTED THE NEXT GUEST ON OUR *FORUMS* AT COMEDY IS DYING DOT COM.

SHE'S A *STELLAR* COMEDIAN WHO JOINED ME THIS PAST SUMMER ON THE *"GET WOKE OR DIE BROKE"* TOUR.

LET'S GIVE A *BIG* C.I.D. WELCOME FOR...

...MY GOOD FRIEND, AVIGAIL SAPPERSTEIN! HOW'S IT *GOING*, AVI?

WOW! AVI! LITERALLY *NOBODY* CALLS ME THAT. THANKS, SNELSON. HAPPY TO BE HERE!

AVIGAL SAPPERSTEIN — STAND-UP COMEDIAN

SO, ON THIS SHOW AND ON OUR WEBSITE, WE TALK A LOT ABOUT COMEDY. WHAT DO *YOU* THINK?

GOSH, IT'S PRETTY CLEAR *YOU* HAVE SOME THOUGHTS. LET'S CENTER THIS CONVERSATION AROUND YOU.

IT'S *SO* IMPORTANT TO GET THE WHITE MALE PERSPECTIVE. SNELSON, WHAT DO *YOU* THINK ABOUT COMEDY?

WELL, I'VE BEEN PRETTY *CLEAR--*

IS IT *DYING?*

83

WHEN COMEDIANS CAN'T TALK ABOUT WHAT'S ON THEIR MIND, COMEDY'S IN A *BAD* PLACE.

HMMMM. WHY *CAN'T* THEY TALK ABOUT WHAT'S ON THEIR MIND, SNELSON? WHAT, SPECIFICALLY, HAPPENS TO THESE COMEDIANS?

I THINK YOU'VE *SEEN* WHAT HAPPENS. YOU'VE WATCHED CANCEL CULTURE COME FOR ME.

SO YOU SHOULD BE ABLE TO SAY WHATEVER YOU WANT WITH *NO* REPERCUSSIONS? I'M JUST TRYING TO UNDERSTAND.

NO, THAT'S NOT IT.

SOME MIGHT SAY WHITE DUDES JUST CAN'T *HANDLE* IT WHEN OTHERS ENJOY THE SAME FREE SPEECH THEY'VE ALWAYS HAD.

THERE NEEDS TO BE A *CONTRACT* BETWEEN AUDIENCES AND COMEDIANS SO WE CAN EXPLORE ISSUES WITHOUT FEAR OF--

SO, LIKE, A *SAFE SPACE?* I THOUGHT YOU DIDN'T LIKE THOSE.

NO, *THAT'S* NOT IT. I JUST THINK COMEDIANS SHOULDN'T HAVE TO WORRY ABOUT ONE BAD WORD OR PHRASE RUINING THEIR CAREER.

WELL, IT'S *YOUR* SHOW. WHAT EXACT WORD OR PHRASE ARE YOU THINKING OF? WHY DON'T YOU JUST SAY WHAT'S ON YOUR MIND, SNELSON?

BARF.

HI! DID YOU JUST SCOFF AT ME? MY NAME'S AVIGAIL. AND YOU ARE...?

LYNZI IRWIN. I'M A--

HEY! *I* KNOW YOU.

YOU DID THAT VIDEO PROTESTING *BILL COSBY'S* REMOVAL FROM THE COMEDY HALL OF FAME, RIGHT? WHAT WAS IT CALLED, AGAIN?

THAT WAS *THE LYNCHING OF FAT ALBERT.*

THAT'S THE ONE! GOSH, YOU SURE DO HAVE A *LOT* OF OPINIONS, HUH?

MY SUPPORTERS ON FUNDAPUNDIT SEEM TO WANT TO HEAR WHAT I THINK.

I *ESPECIALLY* LIKED THE BIT WHERE YOU SHOWED UP AT THE COMEDY HALL OF FAME. WHAT DID YOU SAY?

IT WAS *SOMETHING LIKE,* "YOU CAN'T JUST..."

WE CAN'T JUST START ERASING PEOPLE FROM THE HISTORY BOOKS!

FOOTAGE FROM
THE LYNCHING OF FAT ALBERT

I THOUGHT THAT WAS REALLY *INTERESTING.*

I'M SURE I HAVE *NO IDEA* WHAT YOU'RE...

HISTORIANS RELITIGATE HISTORY ALL THE TIME. WHY DO YOU WANT TO SILENCE *THEIR* FREE SPEECH?

HEY, UH, WHY DON'T WE GET *BACK* TO THE PODCAST?

SURE THING, SWEETIE. I JUST HAD *ONE* MORE QUESTION FOR SNELSON BEFORE WE GET BACK TO IT.

SURE, FINE. WE'LL PROBABLY HAVE TO *RE-RECORD* THAT WHOLE OPENING ANYWAY.

GOSH, I'M SO *SORRY* ABOUT THAT. ANYWAY, I JUST WANTED TO ASK WHAT YOUR DEAL IS?

WHAT DO YOU...UH, *WHAT?*

YOU HAD A SITCOM PILOT. I HEARD YOU NEARLY HAD A BONG ENDORSEMENT DEAL. OUR *TOUR* WAS GOING WELL.

BUT YOU ALWAYS, *ALWAYS* BLOW IT UP.

YOU COULD HAVE A PERFECTLY FINE CAREER. YOU COULD BE THE CHUCK KLOSTERMAN *KNOW-IT-ALL* ASSHOLE OF STANDUP.

THE GUY NO ONE *LIKES*, BUT THEY *LISTEN* TO. BUT YOU JUST CAN'T DO IT. WHAT'S GOTTEN INTO YOU--

CANCER.

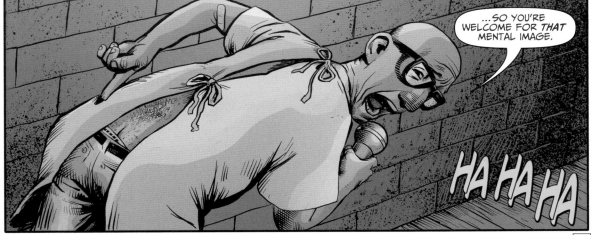

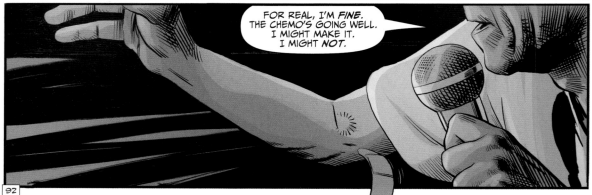

WHETHER I SURVIVE MY ASS CANCER OR NOT DOESN'T HAVE A LOT TO *DO* WITH ME. IT'S NOT UP TO ME.

PEOPLE CALL ME *'BRAVE,'* BUT THAT'S *BULLSHIT.*

I'M LITERALLY NOT FIGHTING *ANYTHING.*

CHEMO'S JUST SITTING MY DISEASED *ASS* IN A CHAIR, WATCHING *'FULL HOUSE.'*

THE FOLKS WHO TAKE CARE OF ME ARE THE BRAVE ONES. THEY SEE THIS DAY *IN* AND DAY *OUT* AND...

I'M *SORRY,* I JUST... I...

WHO KNEW AN ASS FULL OF CANCER WOULD TURN ME INTO SUCH A FUCKING *PUSSY?*

HA HA HA HA

A LOOSE 15 MINUTES LATER...

I THANK YOU FROM THE BOTTOM OF MY CANCER-RIDDEN *ASSHOLE,* NEW YORK!

BEST SHOW *YET!* THAT BREAKING BAD BIT KILLED.

AW, *THANKS,* CALVIN! YOU GUYS UP FOR A REUBEN RUN?

CAN WE DO *FLOYD'S?* THEY HAVE THIS MUSHROOM-BASED MEATLESS PASTRAMI THAT'S ACTUALLY PRETTY--

WE GET IT, AVIGAIL. *CONGRATULATIONS.* YOU'RE A VEGAN.

DONNA'S JUST *JEALOUS* BECAUSE I'M GETTING MORE MEAT THAN SHE IS THESE DAYS.

MY OFFER STANDS. BUY ME A VEGAN REUBEN AND I'LL EAT IT, WITH *ZERO* COMPLAINTS.

94

OKAY, THIS IS FUCKING *GROSS.*

YOU KNOW THE DEAL, DONNA. I BUY IT, *YOU* DON'T WHINE.

I'VE HONORED THAT DEAL THROUGH DOZENS OF DRY-AS-SHIT *GARDENBURGER PUCKS.* BUT COME ON...

...HOW DO YOU MAKE SOMETHING THIS *GUMMY* WITHOUT, LIKE, A POWDER OF CRUSHED HORSE HOOVES?

CRUELTY-FREE GELATIN IS ACTUALLY PRETTY *GOOD.* IN FACT, I THINK IT'S ON THE MENU HERE.

ALL *RIGHT,* YOU TWO. CAN I JUST TAKE A MINUTE, HERE?

YOU'VE ALL BEEN THERE FOR ME OVER THE LAST YEAR, AND I JUST WANT TO *THANK* YOU FOR IT.

HERE WE GO. CHEMO-BRAIN SNELSON'S ABOUT TO GET ALL MISTY.

JUST SHUT THE FUCK UP AND TOAST TO *FRIENDSHIP,* OKAY?

CHEERS!

SO HOW'S THE *MEMOIR* COMING ALONG?

UGH, DON'T *REMIND* ME. I HAVE TO TURN IN A DRAFT TOMORROW.

I THINK IT'S PRETTY COOL. FOR *ONCE*, YOU'RE GETTING PAID TO BE SINCERE.

WELL, THEY DON'T WANT ME TO BE *TOTALLY* SINCERE, DO THEY?

I CAME UP DURING THE 90s, THE *"YEAH, RIGHT"* DECADE. NOBODY WANTS THE *REAL* ME.

THEY WANT CYNICISM WITH A GLOSS OF *NICEY-NICE* ON TOP.

I DISAGREE.

YOU *THINK?* I TOLD CALVIN THE PREMISE SEEMED LIMITED, BUT HE--

WE'VE GOT FIVE EPISODES IN THE CAN, AND THERE'S A LOT OF *GREAT* BUZZ BEHIND IT!

FUNNY, SNELSON, I ALWAYS THOUGHT *LOSS OF APPETITE* WAS A THING WITH CHEMO...

...BUT YOU WENT DOWN ON THAT REUBEN LIKE SHE WAS *BEGGING* FOR IT.

CHEMO AFFECTS PEOPLE *DIFFERENTLY.* MY DOCTOR SAID I'M ONE OF THE LUCKY ONES.

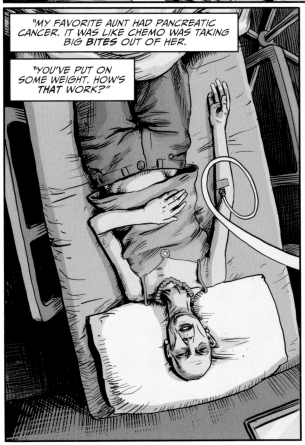

"MY FAVORITE AUNT HAD PANCREATIC CANCER. IT WAS LIKE CHEMO WAS TAKING BIG *BITES* OUT OF HER.

"YOU'VE PUT ON SOME WEIGHT. HOW'S *THAT WORK?"*

IF YOU'RE GONNA FAT-SHAME THE *DYING* GUY, I THINK THE EVENING'S OVER.

SURE. YOU'VE GOT A *BIG DAY* WITH YOUR BOOK TOMORROW, AFTER ALL...

MELVILLE! CAN I *TALK* TO YOU?

YOU REMEMBER ME, RIGHT? *DANICA BAKSHI?* I WAS HOPING I COULD GET FIVE MINUTES OF YOUR--

SORRY, I CAN'T DO *AUTOGRAPHS* RIGHT NOW BECAUSE OF GERMS...

THAT'S OKAY. I JUST HAD A COUPLE OF *QUESTIONS.*

AHHHH! LEAVE ME ALONE!

--TIME?

CHOOIIIICE!

KLANG

ARE YOU--ARE YOU STILL--STILL AT *ALLBIRDS* MAGAZINE?

NO, THEY PIVOTED FROM JOURNALISM TO RENEWABLE *ARCH* SUPPORTS.

RIGHT NOW I'M WRITING *CONTENT* FOR A NEWS-FORWARD VERTICAL SPONSORED BY CAMPBELL'S SOUP.

SOME PEOPLE ≡PHOO≡ HAVE TOO MUCH FUCKING MONEY.

YOU'RE TELLING ME! IT'S CALLED *"M'M! M'M! NEWS!"*

BEER CHIPS Great Goodz CONVENIENCE BANANAS 99¢ VEGANS

HA! THAT'S PRETTY GOOD!

GLAD THE CORPORATE *LOOTING* OF MY PROFESSION AMUSES YOU. SO ANYWAY...

I'M SORRY TO *ASK* THIS, BUT I THINK YOU KNOW I HAVE TO.

MELVILLE SNELSON, DO YOU *REALLY* HAVE CANCER?

REC●

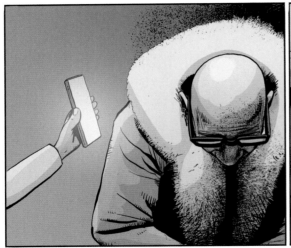

NO, I DON'T.

I HAD A *LUMP* IN MY ASSHOLE. THAT'S TRUE. TURNED OUT TO BE A BENIGN ADENOMA.

WHY DID YOU *LIE*?

SEEMED LIKE A GOOD IDEA AT THE TIME. HOW'D YOU FIND OUT?

SOMEONE LEAKED YOUR MANUSCRIPT. IT WAS *FULL* OF INACCURACIES.

URGENT CARE CLINICS DON'T *DO* CHEMOTHERAPY, FOR ONE THING .

GUESS I *WAS* PRETTY SLOPPY. BUT, LISTEN...

...THEY GAVE ME A PRETTY GOOD ADVANCE. YOU CAN HAVE IT *ALL* IF THIS STORY GOES AWAY.

MELVILLE, ARE YOU TRYING TO *BRIBE* ME?

YOU REALIZE I'M *RECORDING* RIGHT NOW?

I'M SORRY! I'M *SORRY!* I DUNNO WHAT I WAS THINKING.

YEAH, THAT'S OBVIOUS.

REALLY DISAPPOINTING, SNELSON. I DON'T KNOW WHY, BUT I EXPECTED BETTER FROM YOU.

STORY GOES UP NEXT *WEEK*. SEE YOU AROUND.

OKAY. S-SEE YOU.

EXCUSE ME, ARE YOU...MELVILLE SNELSON?

‡SNNNRRRF‡ YEAH?

YOU DON'T *KNOW* ME, BUT MY NAME'S VIVIENNE. AND I JUST WANTED TO THANK YOU.

UHHH, WHAT FOR?

THE WEEK I STARTED CHEMO, I SAW YOU AT THE CELLAR. IT WAS THE *FIRST* TIME I LAUGHED IN MONTHS.

UH, WELL, THAT'S MY *JOB*.

IT WASN'T JUST THE JOKES. YOU *UNDERSTOOD* WHAT I WAS GOING THROUGH.

LOOK, I NEED TO *TELL* YOU...

I DON'T WANT TO TAKE UP *TOO* MUCH OF YOUR TIME. I JUST WANT TO SAY...

...*THANK* YOU.

YOU'RE...YOU'RE *WELCOME.*

113

UH, *THANKS?*

I *GUESS?*

ANYWAY, WHAT WAS I SAYING?

RIGHT! SO HERE'S THE THING...

EVERYTHING'S *SUBSCRIPTION*-BASED NOW! YOU USED TO BUY ALBUMS AND DVDs--

THIS BIT WASN'T FUNNY IN *2012!*

OKAY. BECAUSE I *HATE* MYSELF, I WENT OUT FOR FROZEN YOGURT LAST WEEK...

THAT'S FROM 2010!

...EVER WONDER WHAT *AYN RAND* WOULD THINK OF MR. ROGERS?

LIKE *TWENTY* YEARS OLD, DUDE!

=KOFF=

AW, WHAT'S WRONG? YOU HAVE PRETEND *LUNG* CANCER NOW, TOO?

HA HA HA HA

CHOKING VICTIM

OKAY, GET IT *OUT* OF YOUR SYSTEM. I'M THE IDIOT WHO PRETENDED HE HAD ASS CANCER.

IS THAT THE *BEST* YOU GOT?

CHOKING VICTIM

ASK: Are you choking?

HA HA HA HA HA

LET'S CANCEL CULTURE

THANK YOU. I'M MELVILLE SNELSON, AND YOU'RE LITERALLY THE *WORST* AUDIENCE I'VE EVER HAD.

I COULD USE SOME *ROUGHAGE.* NEXT WEEK, THROW A COBB SALAD.

EXIT

KNOCKED 'EM *DEAD* AGAIN, SLUGGER!

KASHIR, THESE *CHILI CHEESE FRIES* SMELL LIKE RANCID MEOW MIX.

ENTRANCE

SNELSON, YOU'RE A GREAT BRINGER-- THEY LOVE TO *HATE* YOU. BUT A FOOD CRITIC, YOU ARE NOT.

CALL AN *AMBULANCE,* WILLYA? I THINK I GOT SOME IN MY MOUTH!

BUSTER'S COMEDY

TONIGHT'S LINE-UP

JAY MOHR SHOW TIMES MON. 8PM

MARK NORMAND TUES 8PM

KEVIN HART WED 8PM

ANDREW DICE CLAY THURS 8PM, 10PM, 12 AM

FRI

MELVILLE SNELSON 8PM, 10PM, 12 AM SAT 8PM, 10PM, 12 AM

LET'S CANCEL CULTURE

SEE YOU *NEXT* WEEK?

UNFORTUNATELY.

HEY, MELVILLE.

IF YOU WANT TO *PELT* ME WITH KEBABS, YOU HAVE TO PAY AT THE DOOR.

SEEMS LIKE A WASTE OF A *KEBAB.*

AVI! WHAT ARE... WERE YOU *WAITING* FOR ME?

AGAIN, LITERALLY *NOBODY* CALLS ME AVI. WE NEED TO TALK.

I'D HEARD YOU WERE DOING *BRINGER* SHOWS, BUT I DIDN'T QUITE BELIEVE IT.

OPPORTUNITIES KINDA *DRIED* UP, AFTER...

AFTER THE *"CANCER,"* YOU MEAN?

WHAT DO YOU *WANT*, AVIGAIL?

AGAIN, YOUR NON-APOLOGY IS MORE *HORRIFYING* THAN THE ACTUAL CANCER HOAX.

I DON'T HAVE TO *LISTEN* TO THIS.

ACTUALLY, YOU KINDA *DO*. I'M NOT HERE TO YELL AT YOU ABOUT THE FAKED ASS CANCER...

...IS A SENTENCE THAT I ACTUALLY JUST SAID ALOUD.

ANYWAY, I'M HERE BECAUSE OF YOUR *WEBSITE*--YOUR LITTLE MESSAGE BOARD.

COMEDY IS DYING?

YOU HAVE ANY *OTHER* WEBSITES I SHOULD KNOW ABOUT?

I NEED YOU TO CALL OFF YOUR MISOGYNIST *TROLL* ARMY.

MY... *WHAT?*

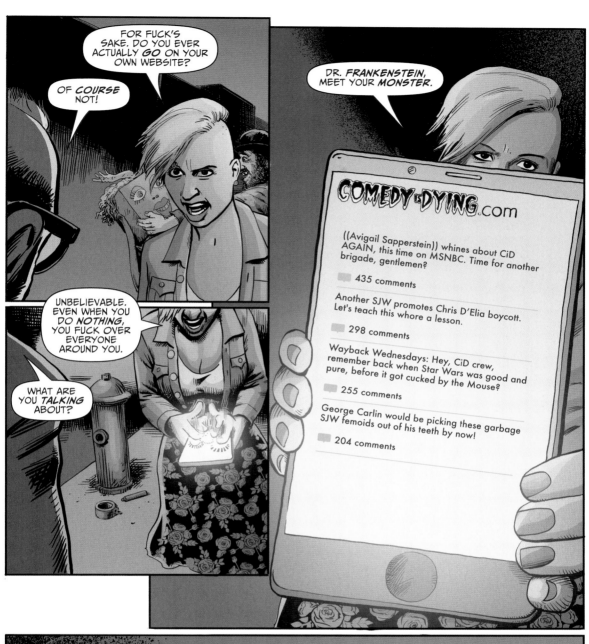

FOR FUCK'S SAKE. DO YOU EVER ACTUALLY *GO* ON YOUR OWN WEBSITE?

OF *COURSE* NOT!

DR. *FRANKENSTEIN,* MEET YOUR *MONSTER.*

COMEDY IS DYING.com

((Avigail Sapperstein)) whines about CiD AGAIN, this time on MSNBC. Time for another brigade, gentlemen?

💬 435 comments

Another SJW promotes Chris D'Elia boycott. Let's teach this whore a lesson.

💬 298 comments

Wayback Wednesdays: Hey, CiD crew, remember back when Star Wars was good and pure, before it got cucked by the Mouse?

💬 255 comments

George Carlin would be picking these garbage SJW femoids out of his teeth by now!

💬 204 comments

UNBELIEVABLE. EVEN WHEN YOU DO *NOTHING,* YOU FUCK OVER EVERYONE AROUND YOU.

WHAT ARE YOU *TALKING* ABOUT?

IT'S THE *SCUMMIEST* PLACE ON THE INTERNET. THEY RUN HARASSMENT CAMPAIGNS AGAINST WOMEN.

WHAT'S A *"PEDE ARMY"?* DO I WANT TO KNOW?

119

PROBABLY NOT. YOUR *RADICALIZED VIRGINS* CHASED ME OFF INSTAGRAM. TWICE.

WOW, THAT *SUCKS.*

I HEAR A *"BUT"* COMING, AND I REALLY *SHOULDN'T* BE HEARING A "BUT" COMING...

BUT THIS SITE'S MY ONLY *INCOME* RIGHT NOW. THE AD DOLLARS KEEP ROLLING IN.

THEY *SWATTED* TABITHA TRAN. SOMEONE COULD'VE DIED.

I GET THAT IT *SUCKS.* REALLY. I'M *WEARING* SOME ASSHOLE'S DINNER RIGHT NOW.

COMEDY IS *TOUGH!* BESIDES, THEY AREN'T EVEN HECKLING YOU IN REAL LIFE. IT'S JUST THE INTERNET.

"JUST THE INTERNET"? I GET *DEATH* THREATS! THESE CHUDS WRITE STORIES ABOUT RAPING ME!

"JUST THE INTERNET," YOU CANCEROUS *ASSHOLE?* YOU THUNDEROUS FUCKING TURD! DON'T YOU GET IT?

H-HEY!

OH, SHIT! *MELVILLE*, ARE YOU OKAY?

AGH! MY *WRIST*!

AVIGAIL! SNELSON! WHAT HAPPENED?

YOUR FUCKING *GIRLFRIEND* JUST BROKE MY FUCKING WRIST, CALVIN!

SHE'S REALLY *UPSET* ABOUT YOUR SITE...

HE DOESN'T *GIVE* A SHIT. OF COURSE.

WE'RE GOING TO GO *COOL OFF*. WE'LL TALK LATER, MAN.

YEAH, *THANKS* FOR NOTHING!

OH, HEY, ALL THIS ASIDE, I'M SORRY TO HEAR ABOUT *GEOFF SARGENT*. I KNOW HE WAS YOUR PAL.

WAIT...

...WHAT *HAPPENED* TO GEOFF SARGENT?

ALT-RIGHT COMEDIAN GEOFF SARGENT KILLS SELF

Alt-right comedian Geoff Sargent was found dead in his Brentwood apartment, an apparent suicide, STARFUCKERZ.COM has exclusively learned. Sargent, who rocketed to fame during the "pickup artist" craze of the mid-2000s, made his name as a provocateur—once chasing Greta Thunberg around a hotel lobby while dressed as the Joker, which he later described as performance art about the futility of the fight against climate change. Sargent recently recanted his most odious political leanings in an apology tour to promote his memoir, "The Third Milkshake."

STILL GOT SOME PAINKILLERS FROM MY ASS GURSERY.

SUR... SURGERY.

C'MON, PILLS. PILLS. AH! THERE YOU ARE.

GRRR!

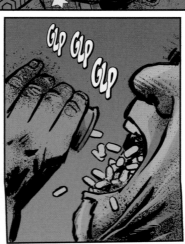

GLP GLP GLP

NLP NLP NLP

SNELSON! *WAKE* UP!

AH!

I'VE BEEN DEAD FOR A YEAR AND I'M *STILL* MAKING EXCUSES FOR YOUR LATE ASS.

MARGE? BUT HOW? I WENT TO YOUR FUNERAL!

DON'T BULLSHIT ME. YOU SKIPPED MY FUNERAL TO DO A SHOWCASE GIG ON LONG ISLAND.

ANYWAY, LET'S GO FOR A WALK.

YOU WANT ME TO CLIMB DOWN THERE?

WE GOTTA GO, KID. I DON'T WANNA KEEP YOU ON YOUR TOES FOREVER.

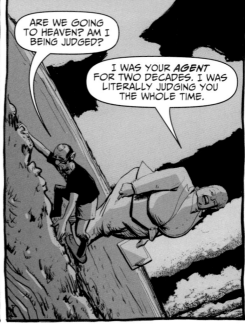
ARE WE GOING TO HEAVEN? AM I BEING JUDGED?

I WAS YOUR *AGENT* FOR TWO DECADES. I WAS LITERALLY JUDGING YOU THE WHOLE TIME.

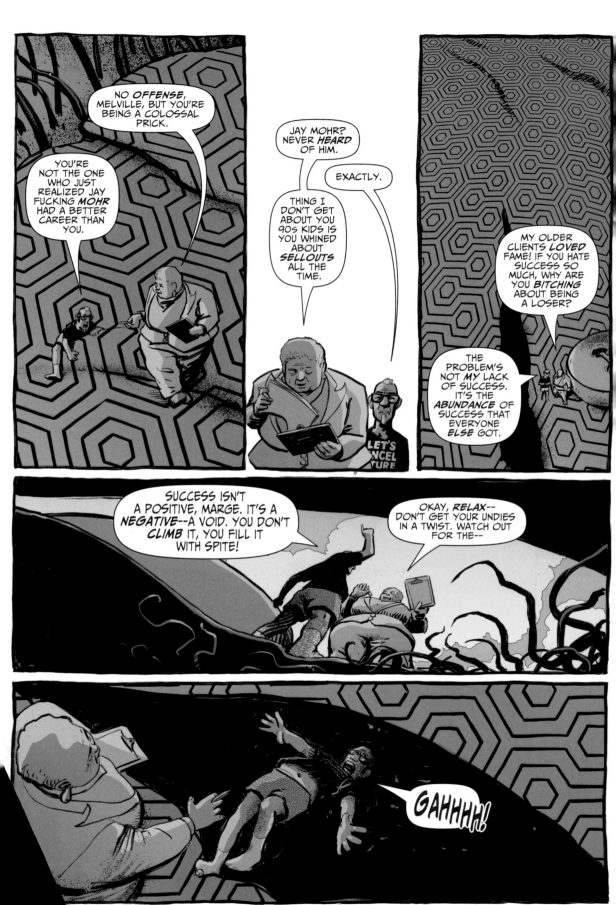

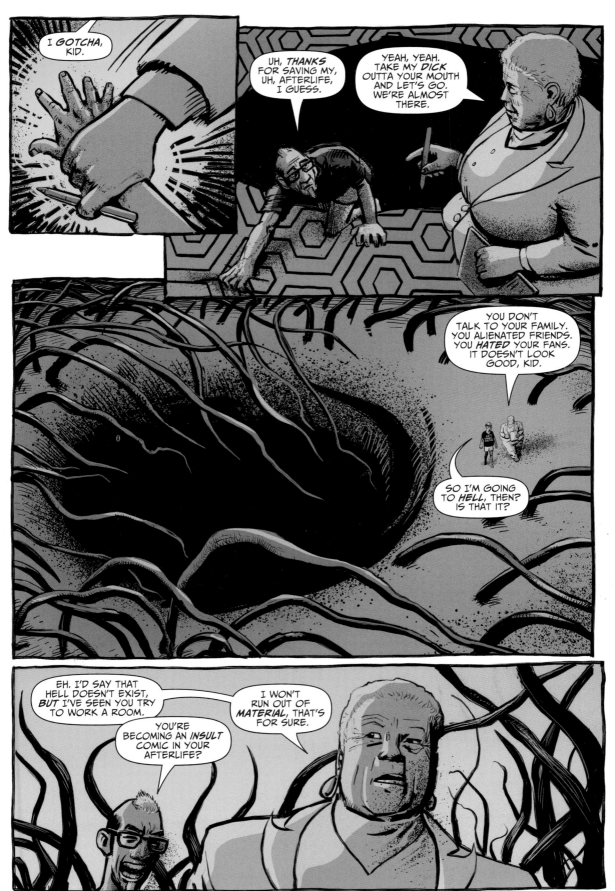

CAN YOU TELL ME *THIS*, THEN? WAS I EVER FUNNY?

YOU *USED* TO BE...

...WHEN I TOOK YOU ON AS A CLIENT. BEFORE YOU LOST PATIENCE AND STARTED CHASING LAUGHS.

YOU FORGOT THAT SOMETIMES THE BEST PUNCHLINE IS NOTHING BUT A *BLANK LOOK* ON SOME RUBE'S DUMB FACE.

YOU'VE GOTTA GET IT INTO YOUR HEAD, MELVILLE: IT'S NOT WHAT YOU THINK OR WHAT PEOPLE THINK OF YOU...

...IT'S WHAT YOU *DO* THAT MATTERS.

NOW DO ME A FAVOR AND *PUKE* ONE MORE TIME, OKAY?

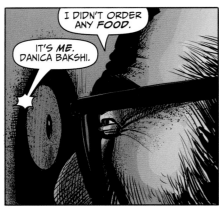

I DIDN'T ORDER ANY *FOOD*.

IT'S *ME*. DANICA BAKSHI.

I KNOW I'M THE *LAST* PERSON YOU WANT TO SEE, BUT I NEED--

--A *QUOTE*?

COME ON *IN*, DANICA.

YOU, UH, HAVEN'T LEFT THE *HOUSE* IN A BIT.

RIDING ON A TIDY LITTLE *SETTLEMENT* I WON BACK IN THE SPRING.

HEARD ABOUT THAT. AVIGAIL SAPPERSTEIN BROKE YOUR WRIST.

SHE PUSHED ME AND THE *GROUND* BROKE MY WRIST.

PROBABLY DOESN'T EVEN *MISS* THE MONEY. SHE'S DRIPPING IN PODCAST CASH.

UH-*HUH*. LISTEN, I'M NOT HERE ABOUT THAT.

I NEED TO ASK YOU ABOUT THE *SHOOTER* IN OHIO.

WHY WOULD I HAVE *ANYTHING* TO SAY ABOUT OHIO? HAVEN'T STEPPED OUTSIDE IN MONTHS.

YOU MEAN YOU HAVEN'T *HEARD?* OH, BOY...

"...LAST NIGHT, AN **ARMED MAN** NAMED DANIEL JAMES DILLARD TERRORIZED TITTERS' TEAROOM IN TOLEDO."

THOUGHT-POLICE **LIBTARDS** ARE **KILLING** COMEDY! LOOK AT YOU SELF-SATISFIED SIMPS-- THIS SHIT ISN'T EVEN FUNNY!

IF IT WASN'T FOR THE FAST ACTION OF THE **HEADLINER**...UH, A KAREN VAN DYKE...

OH, **SHIT!** KAREN "**BULL**" DYKE? IS SHE STILL TOURING?

THINK SHE DROPPED THE **NICKNAME**, BUT YES.

I'M SICK OF THESE **DIVERSITY HIRES** TAKING UP SPACE! GEORGE CARLIN WOULD SHIT HIMSELF RIGHT NOW--

"ANYWAY, KAREN...UH... **DEFUSED** THE SITUATION."

NOT ON **MY** WATCH, ALEX P. KEATON!

BLAM

:HUARp:!

"**GOOD** FOR KAREN. BUT WHAT DOES THIS HAVE TO DO WITH ME?"

"WHEN THEY ARRESTED DILLARD, HE KEPT SHOUTING..."

SOCIAL JUSTICE WARRIORS ARE KILLING STANDUP! VISIT **COMEDY IS DYING DOT COM** FOR THE TRUTH!

OH, *NO.*

HE UPLOADED A MANIFESTO TO *YOUR* WEBSITE AN HOUR BEFORE THE INCIDENT AT TITTERS'.

AND SINCE THEN, YOUR SITE HAS LOOKED LIKE *THIS.*

STILL RECORDING

COMEDY IS DYING.COM

Justice for Danny! The (((media))) is trying Daniel James Dillard in the court of public opinion before he gets a fair trial.

735 comments

Sorry, SJW fuckbois, Danny James Dillard did nothing wrong.

672 comments

Let's be honest: If I had the guts, I'd have "done a Danny" a long time ago.

555 comments

TFW a true hero speaks up for wrongly canceled comedy geniuses. Raise a glass to Roseanne, TJ, Bill, Louis...and Danny.

456 comments

I HAVE TO ASK: AS THE *OWNER* OF COMEDYISDYING.COM, DO YOU HAVE A COMMENT?

YEAH. I'M TAKING THE SITE *DOWN.* IMMEDIATELY. AND PERMANENTLY.

WOW. I DIDN'T *EXPECT* YOU TO...

TO DO THE RIGHT THING? I'M A PRICK, SURE. BUT I'M NOT ONE OF THOSE *COLUMBINE* PRICKS.

THAT'S *IT.* IT'S GONE.

AND YOU'RE NOT GOING TO *SELL* THE URL?

COMEDYISDYING.COM IS OFFICIALLY *DEAD.* I KILLED IT. NO MORE INCEL NARNIA. AND YOU CAN *QUOTE* ME.

I *WILL.*

HEY, WHO'S THIS STORY *FOR,* ANYWAY? YOU'RE ALWAYS AT SOME RIDICULOUS NEW MEDIA START-UP.

I GOT *TIRED* OF GETTING LAID OFF, SO I STARTED MY OWN SITE. IT'S GOING PRETTY WELL!

I'M *GLAD* TO HEAR IT, DANICA. YOU'RE A TALENTED JOURNALIST. I *MEAN* THAT.

THANK YOU, SNELSON.

NOW IF YOU'LL *EXCUSE* ME...

"...I HAVE SOME IMPORTANT *WORK* TO GET BACK TO."

OCTOBER

NOVEMBER

KNOCK KNOCKKNOCK

JESUS FUCKING CHRIST-- WHAT *IS* THIS? GRAND CENTRAL STATION?

THIS BETTER BE *GOOD.* I WAS CULTIVATING SOME REALLY NICE BEDSORES... OH.

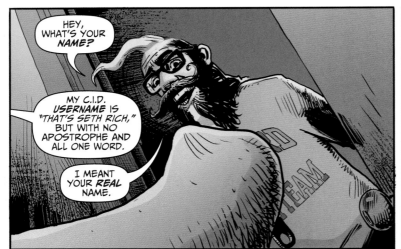

HEY, WHAT'S YOUR *NAME?*

MY C.I.D. *USERNAME* IS "THAT'S SETH RICH," BUT WITH NO APOSTROPHE AND ALL ONE WORD.

I MEANT YOUR *REAL* NAME.

IT'S JAYDEN. JAYDEN *TRILLIN.* I'M FROM MISSOURI.

DID YOU COME ALL THE WAY OUT HERE JUST TO...UH, TO *SEE* ME?

NEVER *BEEN* TO NEW YORK BEFORE.

NEVER BEEN TO *NEW YORK CITY?* LET ME GIVE YOU THE TOUR!

I DON'T *KNOW,* I'M JUST HERE TO...

...OKAY.

PHEW! I MEAN, UH, GREAT!

SO, UH, KAYDEN...

JAYDEN.

RIGHT. YOU REALLY LIKED THE SITE, HUH?

IT WAS THE ONLY PLACE I COULD TURN MY FILTER ALL THE WAY OFF--THE FUNNIEST PLACE ON EARTH!

WOW.

SOME OF THE BEST FRIENDS I'VE EVER MADE WERE ON THAT SITE.

WHEN THAT ONE KID TRIED TO SHOOT UP TITTERS' TEAROOM, I KINDA HAD NO CHOICE.

I JUST CAN'T BELIEVE YOU'RE BOWING TO CANCEL CULTURE.

ARE PEOPLE STILL PRETENDING THAT'S A THING?

WHAT'S A THING?

YOU KNOW, "CANCEL CULTURE."

WHAT ARE YOU TALKING ABOUT? YOU'VE BEEN CANCELED MORE THAN ANYONE!

AND YET, I'M STILL HERE.

143

HEY, THERE'S A GREAT *VIEW* OVER HERE.

AND YOU AREN'T EVEN DOING *STAND-UP* ANYMORE! WHAT'S UP WITH THAT?

I JUST DON'T HAVE *ANYTHING* TO SAY.

NEVER STOPPED YOU *BEFORE.*

HAH!

I WATCHED YOUR OLD SETS ON YOUTUBE. YOU WERE PRETTY *GOOD* IN THE 90s!

YEAH, WELL. *MAYBE.* I USED TO TRY.

WHY'D YOU STOP *TRYING,* THEN? MAN, I'M SO SICK OF PEOPLE QUITTING.

WINNER — BEST DOCUMENTARY — SALT LAKE CITY FILM FESTIVAL

GEOFF SARGENT WAS A BOUNDARY-PUSHING COMEDIAN... UNTIL HE STEPPED OVER THE EDGE.

A DOCUMENTARY BY LYNZI IRWIN

FALLEN SARGENT: A FREE SPEECH STORY

YEAH. ME TOO.

145

BLANG

RUN!

HARVARD
2024
METH TEAM

≈WHOO≈ I THINK ≈WHOO≈ WE'RE OKAY.

SO, UH, WHY'D YOU COME FIND ME?

I WORK--WORKED--OUTSIDE ST. LOUIS AT A *GAS STATION.* YESTERDAY, THIS LADY CAME IN...

"YOU COULD SMELL THE *YANKEE CANDLE* ON HER FROM A FURLONG AWAY. SHE ASKED WHERE THE SOUP WAS.

"AND WE ONLY HAD *TWO* TYPES OF SOUP. THERE WAS THE REGULAR OLD PLAIN CHICKEN AND RICE SOUP...

"...AND THEN WE HAD THE *FANCY* CHICKEN AND RICE SOUP.

"I KNEW SHE WAS GOING TO BUY THE FANCY SOUP. *SHE* KNEW SHE WAS GOING TO BUY THE FANCY SOUP. *YOU* KNOW SHE WAS GOING TO BUY THE FANCY SOUP."

"BUT SHE STARED AT THE CANS FOR **FIFTEEN FUCKING MINUTES** BEFORE SHE BOUGHT THE FANCY SOUP. I REALIZED THAT WAS HOW I WAS GOING TO SPEND THE **REST** OF MY LIFE.

"WATCHING RICH **IDIOTS** PRETEND THEY HAVE A CHOICE BETWEEN REGULAR SOUP AND ORGANIC SOUP, WHEN EVERYONE KNOWS BOTH CANS ARE FULL OF THE **SAME SHIT.**

"THERE'S JUST ONE FUCKING **SPIGOT** AT THE SOUP FACTORY THAT SAYS 'LIQUID YELLOW SODIUM PRODUCT' AND IT FILLS BOTH CANS. BUT WE PRETEND ONE IS FOR **BOUGIE NPR DONORS,** AND ONE'S FOR NORMAL PEOPLE.

"AND THEN I REMEMBERED THAT I COULDN'T EVEN GO **HOME** AND RANT ABOUT THIS ON COMEDY IS DYING DOT COM.

"SO I **GOOGLED** YOU, GOT IN MY CAR, AND HERE WE ARE."

ANYWAY, I'M **SORRY.** I'LL HEAD BACK HOME, NOW.

YOU KNOW **WHAT?**

MAYBE WE SHOULD **TALK** FOR A WHILE LONGER.

HI THERE. HAPPY VALENTINE'S DAY. MY NAME IS JAYDEN TRILLIN. YES, JAYDEN.

I KNOW WHAT YOU GEN-X-ERS ARE THINKING. I'M NOT YOUR OLD INTERN JAYDEN WHO *STOLE YOUR JOB* FOR HALF THE PAY.

AND I'M NOT THE JAYDEN WHO'S HARASSING YOUR *DAUGHTER* ON INSTAGRAM, EITHER.

TWO DECADES AGO, MILLIONS OF *FOOT LOCKER SALESBOYS* FUCKED MILLIONS OF *PIERCING PAGODA COUNTERGIRLS* BEHIND THE FOOD COURT DUMPSTER.

AND NOW THERE ARE JAYDENS *EVERY-FUCKING-WHERE*. I'M ONE OF THEM. NICE TO MEET YOU.

"JAYDEN" IS LATIN FOR "HE WHOSE MOM WAS SLIGHTLY TOO CHRISTIAN FOR SEX WORK."

I'D *HEARD* YOU WERE BACK IN CIRCULATION, BUT I ALMOST DIDN'T BELIEVE IT.

HEY, DONNA! HAVEN'T SEEN YOU SINCE...UH...

SINCE YOU WERE PRETENDING TO HAVE *ASS CANCER.* TIME FLIES. CAN I SIT?

PLEASE.

HEARD YOU WERE *MANAGING* NOW. THE KID'S OKAY.

HE COULD BE *INTERESTING* ONE DAY.

HOW'D YOU *FIND* HIM?

HE WAS GONNA *MURDER-SUICIDE* ME, BUT I CONVINCED HIM TO TRY *STAND-UP* INSTEAD.

THE SAME *END* RESULT, JUST A LITTLE SLOWER GETTING THERE.

HA. I *GUESS.*

THIS IS HIS *FIRST* PAYING GIG. I'M HERE FOR MORAL SUPPORT.

AND I'M SURE YOU'LL COLLECT A *PERFECTLY REASONABLE* FEE FOR YOUR SERVICES.

JUST INDUSTRY STANDARD. *FORTY-FIVE* PERCENT.

YOU'RE STILL AN *ASSHOLE,* SNELSON. IT'S GOOD TO SEE YOU.

YOU *TOO.*

HEY, DO YOU, AH, KEEP IN *TOUCH* WITH THE OLD GANG FROM THE TOUR?

MM-HMM

COOL. I JUST WAS *WONDERING,* UH...

IF YOU EVER SEE AVI AGAIN, COULD YOU TELL HER, AH...

COULD YOU TELL HER I'M *SORRY?* ABOUT THE LAWSUIT AND EVERYTHING AND, I DUNNO, STUFF?

"*SORRY?*" DON'T TELL ME YOU FOUND *JESUS*, OR TOM *CRUISE*, OR SOME OTHER BORING BRUNETTE.

NAH. I JUST THINK MR. TRILLIN HERE WOULD BE A *PERFECT* GUEST FOR AVI'S PODCAST...

I'M SO *RELIEVED* TO LEARN THAT YOUR CONTRITION HAS A SLIMY PROFESSIONAL ANGLE.

ADMIT IT: YOU'D HAVE BEEN *SAD* IF I'D GOTTEN MURDER-SUICIDED TO DEATH.

SURE. AS LONG AS *YOU'RE* ALIVE, NOBODY CAN TELL *ME* I'M THE WORST PERSON IN COMEDY.

SPEAKING OF WHICH, CAN I ASK SOME *ADVICE?* DO YOU THINK IT'S TOO SOON TO DO A *COMEBACK TOUR?*

THANK YOU, NEW YORK! YOU'VE BEEN A FANTASTIC AUDIENCE. GOOD NIGHT!

THE END

154

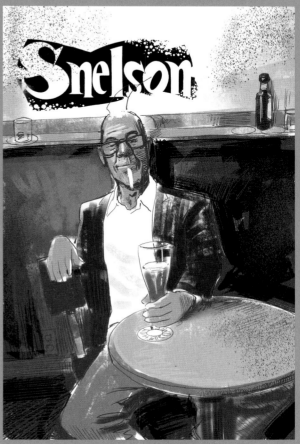

BIOGRAPHIES

PAUL CONSTANT has written journalism, criticism, and essays for the *Los Angeles Times*, *BuzzFeed*, the *Seattle Times*, *Business Insider*, *i09*, *Literary Hub*, and many other publications. His debut comic for AHOY with artist Alan Robinson, *PLANET OF THE NERDS*, was optioned for feature film development by Paramount Players. Find him online at paulconstant.com.

FRED HARPER has illustrated stories for DC Comics and Marvel Comics. Most memorable (at least to Fred) would be penciling for *Animal Man* at DC Vertigo. He started out with *Savage Sword of Conan*, *Ghost Rider*, and *Doctor Strange* at Marvel Comics. He went on to do illustrations for White Wolf and Magic the Gathering as he transitioned to magazine illustrations for *The New York Times*, *The Wall Street Journal*, *Time*, *The Week*, *SPORT*, *The Sporting News*, *Muscle and Fitness*, *Men's Health*, *Muscular Development*, and *Sports Illustrated*... to name a few. Fred currently resides in an apartment where he conducts experiments about the effects of copious amounts of espresso on an artist's brain. Results have been inconclusive, but sometimes secrets take time for the beans to spill.

LEE LOUGHRIDGE is a color artist who has created award-winning work for Marvel, DC, Dark Horse and Image Comics throughout his 25-year career.

ROB STEEN is the illustrator of *Flanimals*, the best-selling series of children's books written by Ricky Gervais, and *Erf*, a children's book written by Garth Ennis.

PETER BAGGE has explored society's oddballs and innovators throughout an award-winning career as a cartoonist. His series *Neat Stuff* and *Hate!* starring Buddy Bradley became totems of pessimistic generational angst in the 1980s and '90s whether he liked it or not. Bagge has also edited the legendary *Weirdo* magazine, done a serialized Bat Boy strip for *The Weekly World News* and dismantled the psychology of Spider-Man and the Incredible Hulk in one-shots for Marvel. In recent years, Bagge has focused his attention on a series of historical biographies on subjects from Margaret Sanger to America's Founding Fathers.

SERGIO ARAGONÉS, one of the world's most prolific— and funniest—cartoonists, is nothing short of an institution. Born in 1937 in Spain, his family immigrated to Mexico where Sergio's love for comics grew. He studied architecture and learned pantomime, but his love for cartooning trumped all else and he sold his first work at age seventeen. Since 1963, he has contributed to hundreds of issues of *MAD Magazine* and released over a dozen paperback books. With Mark Evanier, Aragonés' introduced his bumbling barbarian Groo, who has gone on to star in over 180 issues of hilarity.